Introducti

During the 17th century a visitor to Dolg the town as having 'Walls three miles high' Dolgellau's location at the foot of the easte Moel. Three miles high? No, merely 2831ft (863m), but, nevertheless, high enough to shield the town from the prevailing south-westerly winds and precipitous enough to provide a majestic setting for this small market town, whose narrow, winding streets uniquely contain over 200 listed buildings. With its back to Cadair Idris and built of stone and slate, Dolgellau faces the river Wnion, from whose main crossing, Y Bont Fawr, the town and its mountainous backdrop can be seen to perfection. Just to the east of the bridge, the town's second river, the Aran converges with the Wnion, having fallen, in leaps and bounds, from high on Cadair's ridge to the valley below. The Aran was vital to Dolgellau's industrial development, as it was this fast-flowing river which serviced the town's woollen mills and tanneries. Dolgellau's industrial life is, of course, in the past but its streets, buildings, rivers and setting have today made it a centre for tourism. This book aims to cater for the needs of the town's many visitors who wish to explore the town and its locality on foot.

The twenty walks are designed for those who arrive by car or bus with the intention of spending a few hours on a walk, rather than a whole day. Most of the walks are between 1½ and 4 miles in length (the longest is 5½ miles) and they each introduce the visitor to interesting features of the town and its surrounding countryside. The walks enable the visitor to explore places they would otherwise be unlikely to find during a short visit: minor paths which unexpectedly lead to wonderful viewpoints; an old mill tucked away beside a footbridge over the river Aran barely ten minutes from the town-centre; an ancient well in woods just above the Tywyn road out of Dolgellau; an historic settlement located below the cliffs of Mynydd Moel.

Getting to Dolgellau is straightforward, whether by car or by bus. For car-drivers, directions to Dolgellau from nearby towns are provided, as are details of parking places convenient for the walks. For those travelling by public transport, bus routes and route-numbers are listed. The two main starting points for the walks are the Marian Mawr car-park and Eldon Square bus-stop in Dolgellau town centre. A walking route between the car-park and the bus-stop is outlined. A third starting point, in the Cadair Idris foothills above Plas y Brithdir farm, is a short drive from Dolgellau town-centre. The four walks starting there are linked to walks from the Eldon Square bus stop, so that they can also be accessed by those without a car.

The walks in this book vary in length and level of difficulty but can all be undertaken by a reasonably fit person. Some of the walks are specially suitable for children. Walking boots or strong shoes, and waterproof clothing, are recommended. The location of each route is shown on the back cover and a summary of the main characteristics and approximate length of each is shown on a chart on page 42. An estimated duration is also given but it is best to allow longer in order to linger over the many fine views and interesting places visited whilst on the walks. Each walk has a map and description which enables the route to be followed without further help. A weather forecast for this area is available at www.metoffice.gov.uk.

Enjoy your walking!

WALK 1

DOLGELLAU TOWN & COED ABERNEINT

DESCRIPTION This 2-mile walk takes you past Dolgellau's former police station to a magnificent viewpoint above the town. You then descend to cross the Aran river and enter Coed Aberneint, from where there's another good view over Dolgellau. Allow 1½ hours.

START Eldon Square bus-stop (SH 728178). From the Marian car-park walk past Yr Hên Efail tea-rooms to a road. Turn RIGHT, then LEFT and pass Y Sospan restaurant. Go RIGHT, then LEFT to reach Eldon Square bus-stop.

DIRECTIONS Dolgellau can be reached from Porthmadog via the A487/A470, from Barmouth via the A496/A470, from Bala via the A494, from Machynlleth via the A487/A470, and from Tywyn via the A493. Park in the Marian Mawr car-park (SH728179, post-code LL40 1UU) near the town-centre.

BUS SERVICES Buses 35 (from Blaenau Ffestiniog), 38 (from Barmouth), T2 (from Porthmadog and Machynlleth) and T3 (from Barmouth and Bala) serve Dolgellau. All buses stop in Eldon Square.

1 With your back to the bus-stop turn RIGHT then RIGHT again through an arcade. Ignore a road going right then go RIGHT down steps and RIGHT again. Follow the road to Plas Brith (on the left). Turn LEFT into Lombard Street/Y Lawnt. Pass Lon Bobty, or Baker Street, (on the right) and soon arrive at an impressive building with arched windows (on the left). *This is Dolgellau's former police station. It was built in the mid-19thC.*

2 Continue AHEAD to a main road. Cross the road and go LEFT onto a road signposted 'Cader Idris'. Walk uphill, then turn LEFT at a footpath sign. Go up steps and follow a path uphill. Ignore a minor path on the left then walk up steps to a road. Turn LEFT and walk uphill, passing a signpost to Ffynnon Fair (Mary's Well: see Walks 8 and 13) on the left. *There are great views from here over Dolgellau to the summit of Y Garn, one of the Rhinog range.* Pass a wooden gate (on the left) and a track going right. *To the right of this track is the gateway to Coed Ffridd Jêl, National Park woodland open to the public.* Then continue along the road, ignoring a way-marked path going left, and passing Bryn Ffridd house.

3 When the road ends (near Pen y Banc house), continue AHEAD on a bridleway. Walk uphill to a junction of paths alongside a footpath sign pointing over a wooden stile. *Pause here to take in the view, on the left, over the Wnion valley to the distant Aran Mountains.* Cross the stile and follow the path downhill across a field. Go over another wooden stile, then bear HALF-LEFT, ignoring paths to right and left, and follow a grassy path downhill. Soon bear RIGHT alongside a metal fence (on your left). Cross a third wooden stile and go down steps to a road.

4 Turn RIGHT and follow the road uphill past Argraig house, then downhill into a wooded area and over a bridge across a stream. Then bear LEFT again, ignoring a signposted path and a metal gate, both on the right. Join a path going between a wall (on the right) and a metal fence. Pass a ruined building (on your left) and walk over a wooden bridge. *The ruins are the remains of one of Dolgellau's fulling mills (for washing wool and cloth). To the right of the bridge over the Aran river are the stone buttresses which supported the mill's water wheel.*

5 Go through a wooden gate at the bridge-end and enter Coed Aberneint. *This area was acquired by the Woodland Trust/Coed CADW in 2000. Aberneint is an old Welsh word meaning 'junction of streams'. And, indeed, three water-courses meet near here.* Pass a notice-board, walk AHEAD, then go RIGHT up some wooden steps. Continue uphill alongside a metal fence (on the right). Soon, go through a gap in the fence alongside a wooden gate. Then turn LEFT onto the track beyond.

6 Walk downhill, passing two entrances to Coed Aberneint (on the left) and ignoring several minor paths going right. *Pause near the second entrance for another wonderful view over Dolgellau. Go through the entrance and you'll see, on the left, the eastern summit of Cadair Idris as well.* Continue down the track, which soon becomes a road and passes some house driveways (on the left). Ignore a footpath sign pointing right when the road bends left, and pass (on the right) Felin Uchaf, Dolgellau's community garden (see Walk 8).

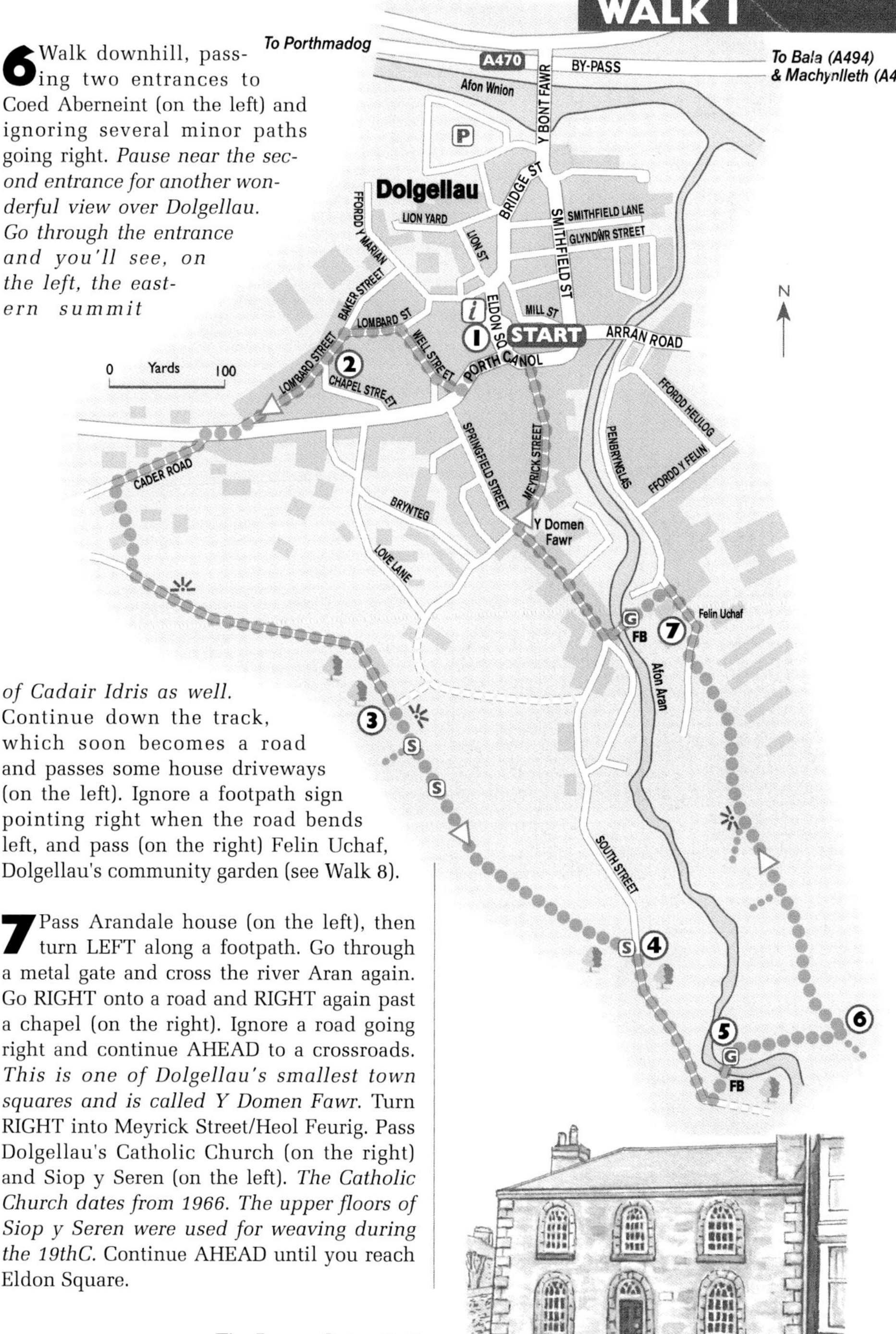

7 Pass Arandale house (on the left), then turn LEFT along a footpath. Go through a metal gate and cross the river Aran again. Go RIGHT onto a road and RIGHT again past a chapel (on the right). Ignore a road going right and continue AHEAD to a crossroads. *This is one of Dolgellau's smallest town squares and is called Y Domen Fawr.* Turn RIGHT into Meyrick Street/Heol Feurig. Pass Dolgellau's Catholic Church (on the right) and Siop y Seren (on the left). *The Catholic Church dates from 1966. The upper floors of Siop y Seren were used for weaving during the 19thC.* Continue AHEAD until you reach Eldon Square.

The Former Police Station

WALK 2

THE RIVER ARAN & PLAS Y BRITHDIR

DESCRIPTION This 2½-mile walk takes you to the remains of a mill on the banks of the river Aran. You climb up through the beautiful forest on the lower slopes of Cadair Idris before following the Aran downhill to the old farm of Plas y Brithdir. You then enjoy glorious views over Dolgellau as you descend to cross the Aran for a third time. Allow 2½ hours.

START Marian Mawr car-park near Dolgellau town-centre (SH 728179). From Eldon Square bus-stop turn LEFT (with your back to the bus-stop) and walk to Lombard Street. Turn RIGHT, then LEFT, past Y Sospan restaurant. Continue AHEAD, then go RIGHT, then LEFT down an alley-way past Yr Hên Efail tea-rooms.

DIRECTIONS Dolgellau can be reached from Porthmadog via the A487/A470, from Barmouth via the A496/A470, from Bala via the A494, from Machynlleth via the A487/A470, and from Tywyn via the A493. Park in the Marian Mawr car-park (SH 728179, post-code LL40 1UU) near the town-centre.

BUS SERVICES Buses 35 (from Blaenau Ffestiniog), 38 (from Barmouth), T2 (from Porthmadog and Machynlleth) and T3 (from Barmouth and Bala) serve Dolgellau. All buses stop in Eldon Square.

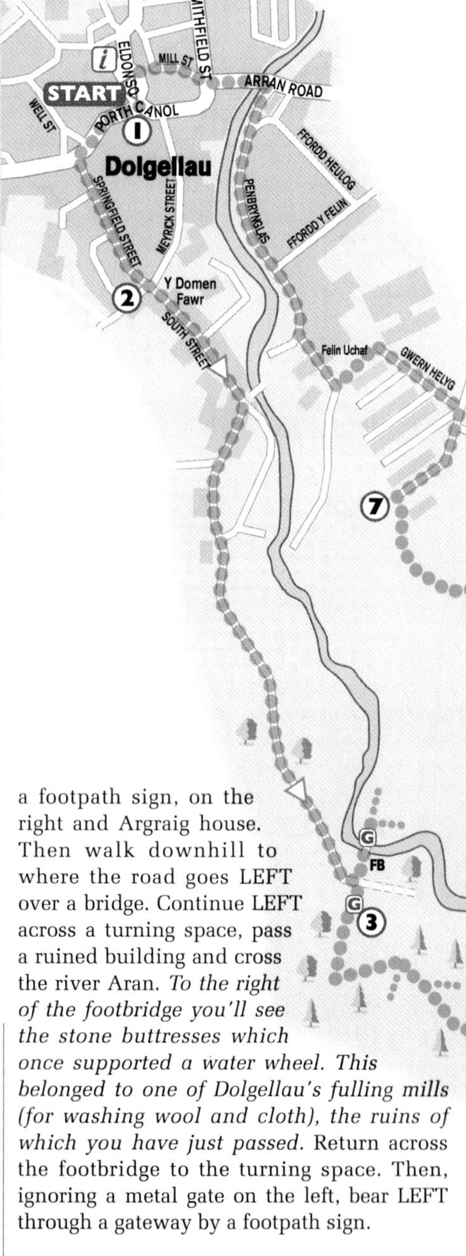

1 With your back to the bus-stop, turn RIGHT, then RIGHT again through an arcade. Continue on the pavement a short distance, ignoring a right-turn and steps going right, then go LEFT into Heol Plas Uchaf/Springfield Street. Follow this uphill to a crossroads with Meyrick Street/Heol Feurig on the left. *This is one of Dolgellau's smallest town squares, Y Domen Fawr.*

2 Continue AHEAD, ignoring a left turn. At the next junction bear RIGHT, following the road uphill. Pass a bridleway sign, then a footpath sign, on the right and Argraig house. Then walk downhill to where the road goes LEFT over a bridge. Continue LEFT across a turning space, pass a ruined building and cross the river Aran. *To the right of the footbridge you'll see the stone buttresses which once supported a water wheel. This belonged to one of Dolgellau's fulling mills (for washing wool and cloth), the ruins of which you have just passed.* Return across the footbridge to the turning space. Then, ignoring a metal gate on the left, bear LEFT through a gateway by a footpath sign.

3 Walk AHEAD then, ignoring way-marked paths going left and ahead, walk RIGHT, following a path initially alongside the stream on the right. Soon the path widens and bears LEFT, continuing uphill. Ignore a path going left, then take the SECOND path going RIGHT after it. Follow this uphill to a wooden gate. Go through and AHEAD. Soon bear LEFT onto a track which comes in through a metal gate on the right. Make for a waymark and continue uphill, passing another waymark. Soon go through a gateway, passing a footpath sign, to a road. Turn LEFT along the road and pass Parc Cottage. *Look to the right here and you'll glimpse the eastern ridge of Cadair Idris.* Soon pass a footpath sign indicating a track going right. ***(Those joining Walk 19, Stage 2 from Walk 2 should go RIGHT onto this track).***

4 Continue on the road, going through a metal gate and uphill. Ignore a track going right to Hafodygoeswen (see Walk 17). Go through the gate next to a cattle-grid and follow the road LEFT over a bridge. You are now crossing the Aran again. ***(Go RIGHT here and uphill to reach the starting point for Walks 17, 18 and 20).***

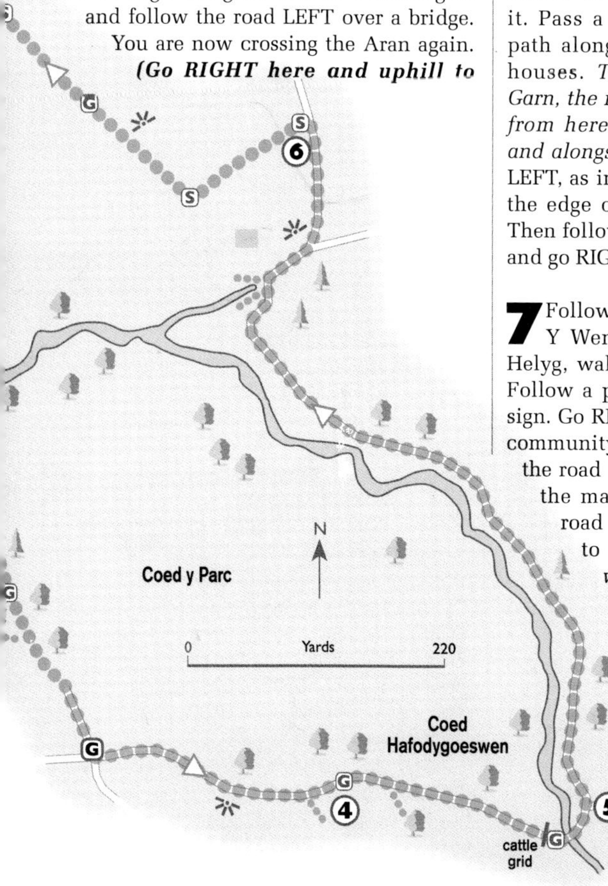

5 Bear LEFT and walk downhill alongside the river, passing the entrance to Dref Gerrig (see Walks 12, 18 and 20) on the right. Soon the road bears sharply RIGHT then LEFT. Ignore a footpath sign pointing left, and walk over a bridge. Go RIGHT past a house. This is the old farm of Plas y Brithdir. Follow the road LEFT at a junction, ignoring a bridleway sign pointing right and the farm entrance. *Pause here for a magnificent view over Dolgellau to the Mawddach Estuary.* Continue downhill and, soon, go LEFT at a waymark and up steps. Cross a wooden stile.

6 Walk AHEAD across a field alongside a fence. Go uphill towards a gate and RIGHT across a wooden stile to the left of it. Pass a waymark and continue down a path alongside a fence, beyond which are houses. *There are wonderful views of Y Garn, the mountain to the north of Dolgellau from here. Soon, walk through a gateway and alongside a fence.* Cross a stile and turn LEFT, as indicated by waymarks. Walk along the edge of a field and cross another stile. Then follow the path down to a footpath sign and go RIGHT onto a road.

7 Follow this downhill past a bus-stop and Y Wenallt. Soon go LEFT onto Gwern Helyg, walking downhill to a footpath sign. Follow a path down to a road and footpath sign. Go RIGHT past Felin Uchaf, Dolgellau's community garden (see Walk 8) and follow the road downhill. Continue AHEAD when the main road goes right, and follow a road alongside the river then bear LEFT to Aran Bridge. *The existing bridge was built on top of the earlier, narrower bridge. This area was once at the centre of Dolgellau's woollen and tanning industries.* Turn LEFT and walk over the bridge to Y Meirionnydd hotel. Then cross the road into Mill Street and follow it past the Cross Keys pub. Turn LEFT by the main pub entrance to reach Eldon Square.

WALK 3

ESGEIRIAU & NANT Y CEUNANT

DESCRIPTION A 2½-mile walk during which you climb the lower slopes of Cadair Idris to Esgeiriau house high above Dolgellau. You then follow a road west across the hillside, where there are glorious views to the north of the town, before crossing the Nant y Ceunant. This precipitous stream and gorge initially runs parallel to the track which then takes you back down to Dolgellau. Allow 2½ hours.

START Eldon Square bus-stop (SH 728178). From the Marian car-park walk past Yr Hên Efail tea-rooms to a road. Turn RIGHT, then LEFT and pass Y Sospan restaurant. Go RIGHT, then LEFT to reach Eldon Square bus-stop.

DIRECTIONS Dolgellau can be reached from Porthmadog via the A487/A470, from Barmouth via the A496/A470, from Bala via the A494, from Machynlleth via the A487/A470, and from Tywyn via the A493. Park in the Marian Mawr car-park (SH 728179, post-code LL40 1UU) near the town-centre.

BUS SERVICES Buses 35 (from Blaenau Ffestiniog), 38 (from Barmouth), T2 (from Porthmadog and Machynlleth) and T3 (from Barmouth and Bala) serve Dolgellau. All buses stop in Eldon Square.

1 With your back to the bus-stop, cross Eldon Square, turn RIGHT, cross the road ahead and walk into Heol Feurig/Meyrick Street. Pass Siop y Seren (on the right) and then the Catholic Church (on the left). *The upper floors of Siop y Seren were used for weaving during the 19thC. The Catholic Church dates from 1966.* Continue AHEAD to a junction. *You are now in one of Dolgellau's smallest town squares, Y Domen Fawr.*

2 Turn LEFT here and continue AHEAD, ignoring a left turn. Take the next road on the LEFT and, soon, go LEFT downhill and over a footbridge. *This takes you across the river Aran, one of Dolgellau's two main rivers.* Go through a metal gate and continue to a road and footpath sign. Turn RIGHT and walk AHEAD, ignoring a road going right. Pass Felin Uchaf, Dolgellau's community garden (see Walk 8), and a footpath sign, both on the left. Follow the road uphill to the entrance to Coed Aberneint (on the right). *Aberneint is an old Welsh word meaning 'junction of streams'. The wood was given this name since three water-courses meet nearby.*

3 Turn RIGHT into Coed Aberneint and follow a narrow path crossing a grassy slope. Bear RIGHT at a junction of paths and soon go downhill. *As you descend, notice the waterfall on the river Aran to your right.* Ignore a path going left as you make for a wooden gate. Go through and cross the Aran on a footbridge. *To the left you'll see the stone buttresses which once supported a water wheel. This belonged to one of Dolgellau's fulling mills (for washing wool and cloth), the ruins of which are on the right after the bridge.* Continue AHEAD to an open space at the end of a road. Cross this, ignoring a metal gate on the left, and walk through a gateway by a footpath sign.

4 Walk AHEAD, then, ignoring waymarked paths going left and ahead, turn RIGHT, following a path initially alongside the stream on the right. Soon the path widens and bears LEFT, continuing uphill. Ignore a path going left, then take the FIRST path going RIGHT after it. Soon this path bears RIGHT, continuing uphill between trees. After some zig-zags, the path arrives at steps leading up to a metal gate in a wall. Go through and AHEAD alongside a stream on the right. Ignore a metal gate into a field (on the left) then a bridge over the stream, continuing uphill to a waymark by a road.

5 Turn RIGHT onto the road and go through a metal gate and across the stream, passing a house on the right. *This is Esgeiriau, a house spectacularly situated overlooking Dolgellau on a spur of the Cadair Idris ridge. Esgair means ridge.* Follow the road over another stream and past the entrance (on the left) to Bryn Mawr house (see Walk 19). Continue to a wooden gate in the wall on the right. *This is a good viewpoint. The mountain to the north of Dolgellau is Y Garn, one of the Rhinog range.* Follow the road downhill then over a bridge to a bridleway sign pointing right.

6 Turn RIGHT through a metal gate and walk along the track beyond. *The stream and gorge on the right is called Nant y Ceunant. The stream makes a precipitous descent to join the Aran river.* Pass a wooden gate (on the right), then walk uphill, ignoring a minor track going left. *To the RIGHT from here you can see the eastern summit of Cadair Idris, Mynydd Moel.* The track levels off then descends towards a wall. Turn RIGHT alongside a tree and go downhill parallel to the wall. Go LEFT through a metal gate and downhill.

7 Go RIGHT to a junction and bridleway sign, then LEFT, walking downhill to a road. Continue AHEAD past houses. Then turn RIGHT at a waymark, go through a kissing-gate and walk downhill to a junction. Turn RIGHT, pass two wooden gates and turn RIGHT onto the road beyond. Follow this LEFT downhill to a cross-roads, Y Domen Fawr. Continue AHEAD, following Meyrick Street/Heol Feurig past the Catholic Church to return to Eldon Square.

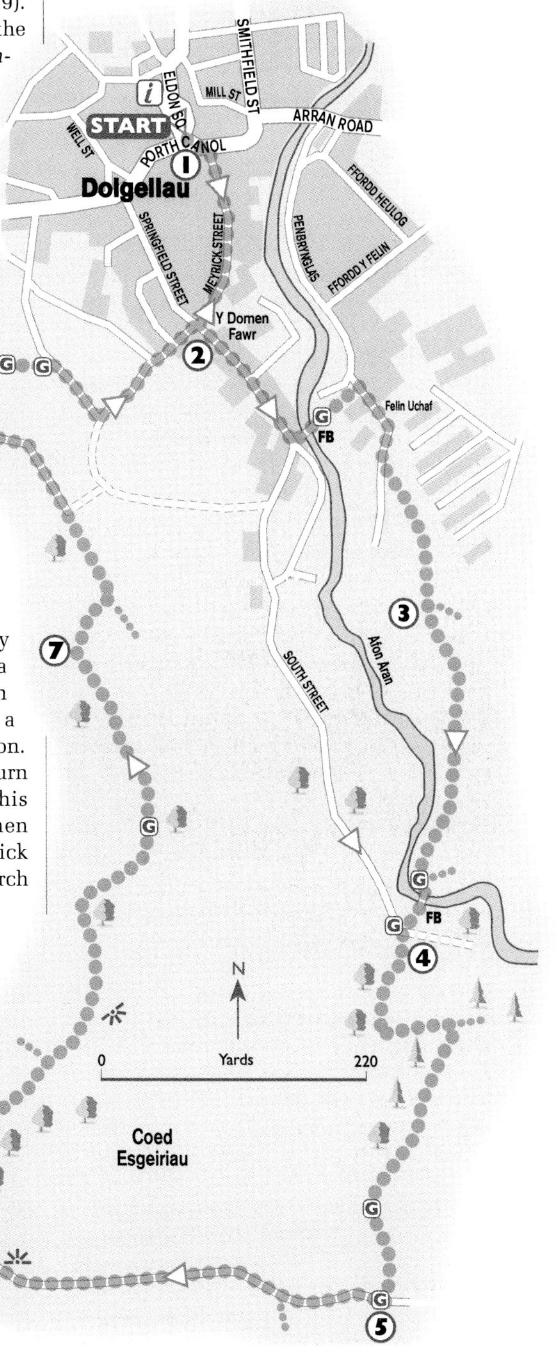

WALK 4

DOLGELLAU RADIO STATION & TYDDYN BACH

DESCRIPTION A 2-mile walk which provides spectacular views of the Cadair Idris mountain ridge from the hills just to the north of Dolgellau. You walk, on a little used road, past the town's strategically placed radio station to the settlement of Tyddyn Bach. Then a delightful path takes you through fields and steeply downhill alongside a stream back to the town. Allow 1½ hours.

START Marian Mawr car-park near Dolgellau town-centre (SH 728179). From Eldon Square bus-stop turn LEFT (with your back to the bus-stop) and walk to Lombard Street. Turn RIGHT, then LEFT, past Y Sospan restaurant. Continue AHEAD, then go RIGHT, then LEFT down an alley-way past Yr Hên Efail tea-rooms.

DIRECTIONS Dolgellau can be reached from Porthmadog via the A487/A470, from Barmouth via the A496/A470, from Bala via the A494, from Machynlleth via the A487/A470, and from Tywyn via the A493. Park in the Marian Mawr car-park (SH728179, post-code LL40 1UU) near the town-centre.

BUS SERVICES Buses 35 (from Blaenau Ffestiniog), 38 (from Barmouth), T2 (from Porthmadog and Machynlleth) and T3 (from Barmouth and Bala) serve Dolgellau. All buses stop in Eldon Square.

1 Walk to the car-park entrance then turn LEFT and cross the bridge over the river Wnion. *Parts of this bridge, called Y Bont Fawr, date from 1638. It was seriously damaged when the Wnion flooded in 1903.* At the end of the bridge turn LEFT then go RIGHT to cross the road at the pedestrian lights. Go LEFT then RIGHT into the first road on the right. Follow this road uphill, ignoring minor roads going to left and right. After a time go through the end of speed limit signs and follow the road RIGHT at a junction where a road signposted for the golf-course (see Walks 5 and 16) goes left. Continue uphill and pass the entrance to the Dolgellau radio station on the right. *The station was built by the BBC and opened as a television transmitter in 1967. It now transmits BBC radio stations. The mast is 22m high.*

2 The road levels off and, before long, you pass a junction where tracks go to the left. *Soon after this junction look left for a good view of the upper Mawddach estuary.* Pass a white metal post with a red top (indicating a gas line crossing) on the right before you arrive at a metal gate and wooden stile (also on the right). Turn RIGHT and cross the stile to walk uphill alongside the boundary of Tyddyn Bach house (on the left). *The views, ahead, of the Cadair Idris ridge are unvaryingly spectacular for the next section of the walk. The summit of the mountain, Penygadair, is the peak towards the centre of the long ridge.*

3 Pass a waymark and walk along a track which descends between trees. Soon, pass a telegraph pole (on the right) and walk through a gap in the wall AHEAD. Beyond this, follow the path going AHEAD towards a wire fence. Cross a wooden stile, alongside a waymark, and follow the path HALF-LEFT away from the fence. The path takes you under telegraph wires towards another telegraph pole. Continue AHEAD, ignoring paths to right and left. Soon, the path bears HALF-RIGHT and heads towards a metal kissing-gate.

4 Go through the gate and cross a stream on a wooden footbridge. After the stream, make for the waymark you can see HALF-RIGHT ahead and pass it, crossing a field and walking towards the right-hand end of a grassy hillock with trees and boulders on it. Here, turn LEFT and walk AHEAD, going downhill across the field towards a stile and a gate in a wall. *The view of Dolgellau and Cadair Idris from here could hardly be bettered. You can see how the town shelters under the spectacular cliffs below Mynydd Moel, the eastern summit of the mountain, and the way in which the long ridge towers above the Mawddach Valley towards the west.* Cross the stile and continue AHEAD downhill to another stile.

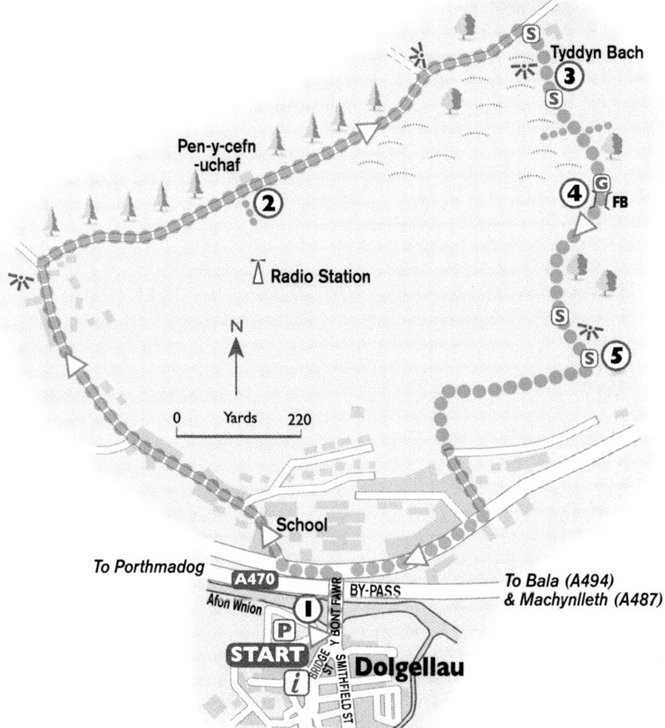

5 Cross this stile and follow the (recently diverted) path RIGHT alongside the wall. After a time, the path goes steeply downhill, using wooden steps. Pass a waymark (on the right) and follow the path LEFT as it continues downhill alongside a stream (on the right). Soon, the path comes to a road. Pass a footpath sign and join the road, walking AHEAD and downhill. Pass a house called Fronallt (on the left) and continue downhill, ignoring roads to left and right, to a main road. Cross the road to the supermarket opposite and turn RIGHT. Walk along the pavement past a petrol station and turn LEFT. Cross the bridge over the Wnion river to return to the starting point.

The Old Courthouse, Dolgellau, now Y Sospan restaurant

WALK 5

CAE CLYD & PENTRE FARM

DESCRIPTION This 2½-mile walk demonstrates just how quickly you can climb from the streets of Dolgellau to fields with glorious views over the town. You pass the ancient site of Cymer Castle and skirt the beautiful upper Mawddach Valley before returning to Dolgellau along a path beside the town's golf course. Allow two hours.

START Marian Mawr car-park near Dolgellau town-centre (SH 728179). From Eldon Square bus-stop turn LEFT (with your back to the bus-stop) and walk to Lombard Street. Turn RIGHT then LEFT, past Y Sospan restaurant. Continue AHEAD, then go RIGHT, then LEFT down an alley-way past Yr Hên Efail tea-rooms.

DIRECTIONS Dolgellau can be reached from Porthmadog via the A487/A470, from Barmouth via the A496/A470, from Bala via the A494, from Machynlleth via the A487/A470, and from Tywyn via the A493. Park in the Marian Mawr car-park (SH 728179, post-code LL40 1UU) near the town-centre.

BUS SERVICES Buses 35 (from Blaenau Ffestiniog), 38 (from Barmouth), T2 (from Porthmadog and Machynlleth) and T3 (from Barmouth and Bala) serve Dolgellau. All buses stop in Eldon Square.

1 Walk to the car-park entrance, go LEFT and across the river Wnion. At the bridge-end go LEFT, then RIGHT over a pedestrian crossing. Go RIGHT, following the pavement past a petrol station (on the right). Turn LEFT into Coed y Fronallt. Follow this road AHEAD. When it goes right by a footpath sign walk AHEAD, following a footpath uphill alongside a stream. Go RIGHT up wooden steps near a waymark. The path then levels off and continues alongside a wall (on the left).

2 Go LEFT over a wooden stile and uphill across a field to a stile and gate in the wall AHEAD. *Pause here and admire the view back over Dolgellau to Cadair Idris. Notice how the town is dominated by the cliffs of the eastern summit of the mountain, Mynydd Moel.* Cross the stile and continue AHEAD, walking past the end of a grassy hillock with trees and boulders on it (on your right). Bear HALF-RIGHT, making for a waymark. Pass this and then walk through trees before crossing a wooden footbridge and going through a metal kissing-gate. Continue AHEAD on a grassy path.

3 Walk under telegraph wires, ignoring paths to right and left, and then cross a wooden stile alongside a waymark. Go through a gap in a wall, then AHEAD, ignoring field entrances to left and right. Follow a trackway uphill between trees to a yellow-topped waymark. Then continue AHEAD, walking to the left of the boundary hedge and fence alongside a house. Cross a wooden stile alongside a metal gate to arrive at a tarmac road.

4 Turn RIGHT and walk past the house. *The house is called Tyddyn Bach.* Continue along the road (which is little used) until you come to a junction. Here, turn LEFT and walk past Pandy Bach house (on the right). Soon a track comes in from the right and you'll pass Cae Clyd house (on the left). *Look up to the right along this stretch of the road and you'll be able to see the hillock, surrounded by trees, which is the site of Cymer Castle. The first recorded mention of the castle was in 1116. It was built overlooking the strategically important Mawddach Estuary. Walk 16 visits Cymer Abbey which is a mile or so away in the Mawddach valley.* Continue along the road as it descends to the valley.

5 Soon, after a sharp left-hand bend, go AHEAD at a junction (the road going right is signposted Cycle Track 82). Then turn LEFT at a footpath sign and walk uphill following the road to Pentre Farm. *There's a wonderful view from in front of the farmhouse down the Mawddach Valley.* Turn LEFT past a metal gate on the left. Then walk to the LEFT of Pentre farmhouse past a barn. Go through a gate and continue AHEAD with a wall and fence on your right. Follow the wall downhill to a metal gate.

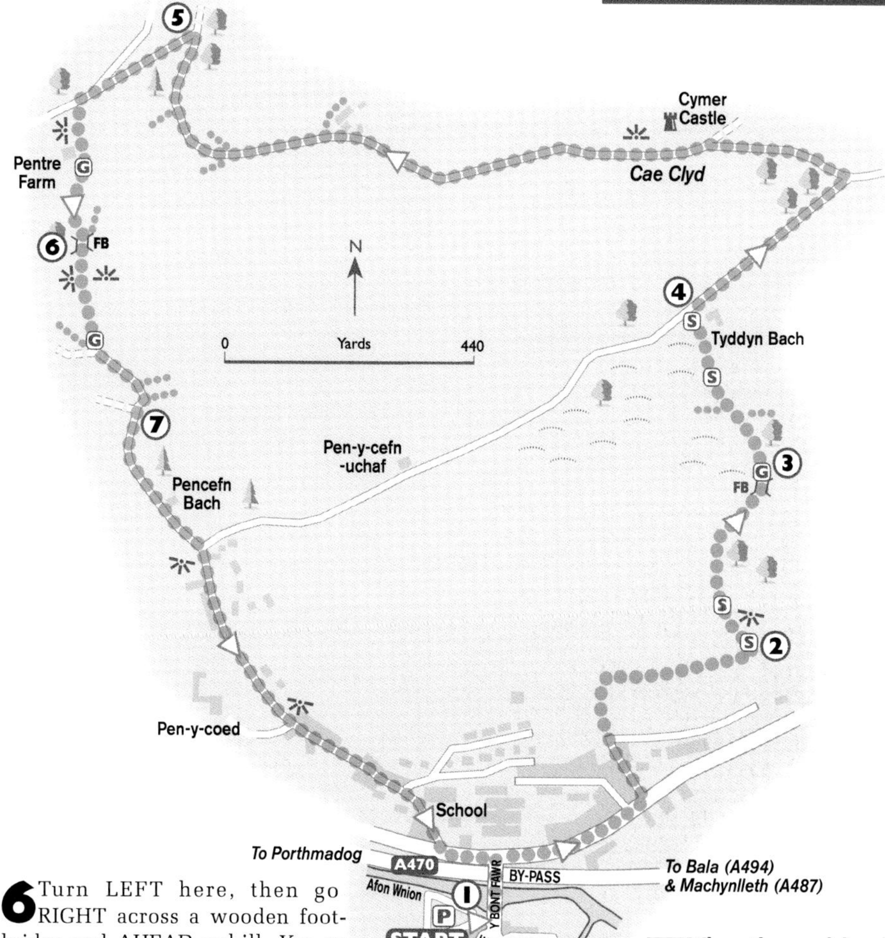

6 Turn LEFT here, then go RIGHT across a wooden footbridge and AHEAD uphill. *You are now on a right-of-way across the Dolgellau Golf Course.* Pass a white gas pipeline marker and, at the top of the hill, a wooden post. *There's another good view down the Mawddach, to the right, here. If you look back the way you have come you'll see the summit of Y Garn, a mountain belonging to the Rhinog range to the north of Dolgellau.* Continue AHEAD alongside the wall and fence (on the right) until you reach a wooden gate. Go through and turn LEFT onto a track opposite the entrance to Hengwrt Cottage. Ignore subsequent tracks going to left and right before passing a footpath sign. Walk AHEAD, passing the golf-club car-park, to join a tarmac road which leads uphill.

7 When the road levels off, pass a house (on the left) before arriving at a road junction. *There is another wonderful view over Dolgellau to the Cadair Idris ridge from this point. A seat is provided.* Turn RIGHT at the junction and follow the road downhill between houses, ignoring minor roads to left and right. *Soon, the centre of Dolgellau comes into view and you'll be able to make out the tower of the parish church (see Walk 9).* After a time pass a school (on the right) and walk downhill to another road junction. Turn LEFT here, then go RIGHT over the pedestrian-controlled crossing. Go LEFT and immediately RIGHT to cross the bridge over the river Wnion and return to the starting point.

WALK 6

PEN Y FRON SERTH & TREFEILIA

DESCRIPTION This 2½-mile walk takes you into the wooded hills to the south-east of Dolgellau, from where there are good views over the town. On the return you cross the Aran river, which flows through the centre of Dolgellau. (A short section of Stage 1 of Walk 6 involves walking along a main road without pavements. This can be avoided by omitting Stage 2: see Stage 1 below.) Allow 2½ hours.

START Eldon Square bus-stop (SH 728178). From the Marian car-park walk past Yr Hên Efail tea-rooms to a road. Turn RIGHT, then LEFT and pass Y Sospan restaurant. Go RIGHT, then LEFT to reach Eldon Square bus-stop.

DIRECTIONS Dolgellau can be reached from Porthmadog via the A487/A470, from Barmouth via the A496/A470, from Bala via the A494, from Machynlleth via the A487/A470, and from Tywyn via the A493. Park in the Marian Mawr car-park (SH 728179, post-code LL40 1UU) near the town-centre.

BUS SERVICES Buses 35 (from Blaenau Ffestiniog), 38 (from Barmouth), T2 (from Porthmadog and Machynlleth) and T3 (from Barmouth and Bala) serve Dolgellau. All buses stop in Eldon Square.

1 With your back to the bus-stop go RIGHT then cross the road ahead. Turn LEFT to join the pavement and follow this out of Eldon Square, crossing the road going right. Pass Y Meirionnydd hotel (on the right) and continue AHEAD across the Aran Bridge. Cross the road again by the entrance to Ysgol y Gader and continue on the left pavement. Cross Doldir and walk AHEAD, passing Fron Serth (on the right) and a garage. *(Go RIGHT and follow Fron Serth to shorten this walk by omitting Stage 2.)*

2 The pavement stops after Dolawel house so walk on the right-hand side of the road for a short distance, passing Tanyfron Holiday Home Park and Felinship Cottage. Take the next road on the RIGHT. Walk over a cattle-grid and cross a stile alongside a footpath sign. Continue AHEAD on the road, climbing steeply. Soon go LEFT and through a metal gate alongside a stile. *Pause here and look back the way you've come for a magnificent view over Dolgellau.* The road then levels off and turns sharply RIGHT. Cross a cattle-grid, then bear LEFT alongside a wooden fence. Pass two metal gates before going LEFT over a wooden stile. Walk AHEAD across a field towards a wall and large tree on your right. *Over to the left you can now see the rounded summit of Foel Offrwm, the site of an ancient hill-fort.* Walk between the wall and a telegraph pole, then make for the gate, stile and footpath sign AHEAD. Cross the stile and turn LEFT onto the road beyond.

3 The road is Fron Serth. Walk uphill past Pen y Fron Serth house, then turn RIGHT onto a bridleway. Ignore right and left turns and follow the main track RIGHT over a cat-

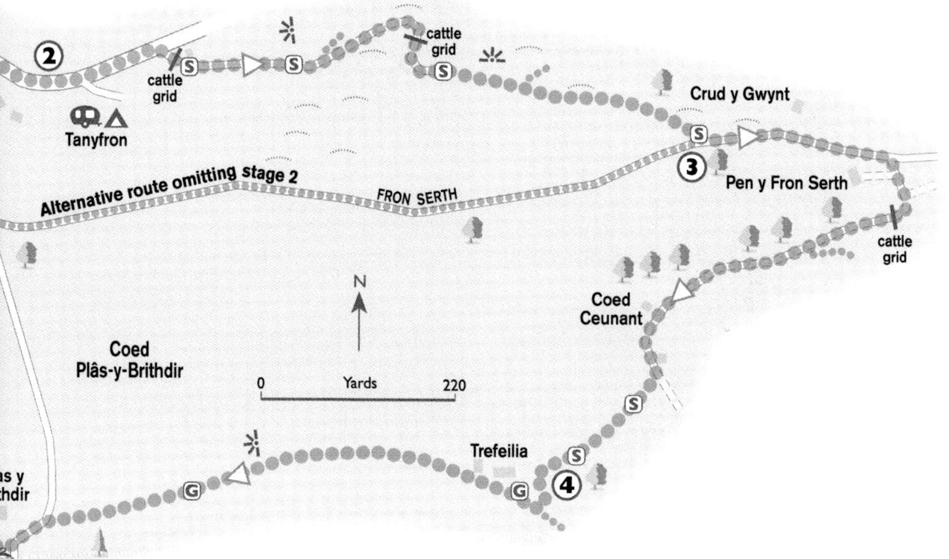

tle-grid. Pass Coed Ceunant house, then bear HALF-RIGHT at a footpath sign and walk downhill to a stile. Cross this and continue alongside a wall and stream. Ignore a gateway (on the left) and walk downhill through trees to a gate and stile. Go over and continue downhill to a waymark.

4 Turn LEFT onto a track which goes RIGHT through a wooden gate and past the settlements of Ysgubor and Trefeilia. Follow the road AHEAD through an old gateway and across fields. *Soon, there are wonderful views down to Dolgellau. You can make out the parish church in the centre of the town (see Walk 9) and the radio station on the hill to the north (see Walk 4).* Soon walk through a metal gate and downhill to a road junction and bridleway sign. Turn LEFT here and pass Plas y Brithdir farm (on the right).

5 Continue AHEAD when the road turns left. Follow a track past Frongoch house and then downhill. Ignore paths and gates to left and right before reaching Coed Aberneint (on the left). *Aberneint is an old Welsh word meaning 'junction of streams'. The wood was given this name since three water-courses meet near the site.* Turn LEFT alongside a wooden gate and walk downhill on a path which ends with a series of steps. Go through the wooden gate AHEAD and across the footbridge over the Aran river. *To the left you'll see the stone buttresses which supported a water wheel. This helped drive machinery at one of Dolgellau's fulling mills (for washing wool and cloth), the ruins of which can be seen on the right.* Ignoring a footpath sign, bear RIGHT onto a road which crosses a bridge and goes uphill.

6 Pass Argraig house (on the left) and walk downhill, ignoring a footpath sign and turns to left and right. Soon arrive at Glan Aran house (on the left). Opposite a bridleway sign, bear RIGHT onto a narrower road and then, at another footpath sign, turn RIGHT and cross another footbridge over the Aran river. Go through a metal gate and AHEAD to a road. Turn LEFT then continue AHEAD when the road divides and walk alongside the Aran. When this road goes right walk AHEAD alongside the river. Turn LEFT across the Aran Bridge and return to the starting point.

WALK 7

PENMAENPOOL & THE CADAIR IDRIS FOOTHILLS

DESCRIPTION A 5½-mile walk which takes you along the Mawddach Valley on the disused railway line from Dolgellau to Penmaenpool. You then climb out of the valley into the foothills of Cadair Idris from where there are magnificent views of the Rhinog Mountains to the north. Allow five hours.

START Marian Mawr car-park near Dolgellau town-centre (SH 728179). From Eldon Square bus-stop turn LEFT (with your back to the bus-stop) and walk to Lombard Street. Turn RIGHT then LEFT, past Y Sospan restaurant. Continue AHEAD, then go RIGHT, then LEFT down an alley-way past Yr Hên Efail tea-rooms.

DIRECTIONS Dolgellau can be reached from Porthmadog via the A487/A470, from Barmouth via the A496/A470, from Bala via the A494, from Machynlleth via the A487/A470, and from Tywyn via the A493. Park in the Marian Mawr car-park (SH 728179, post-code LL40 1UU) near the town-centre.

BUS SERVICES Buses 35 (from Blaenau Ffestiniog), 38 (from Barmouth), T2 (from Porthmadog and Machynlleth) and T3 (from Barmouth and Bala) serve Dolgellau. All buses stop in Eldon Square.

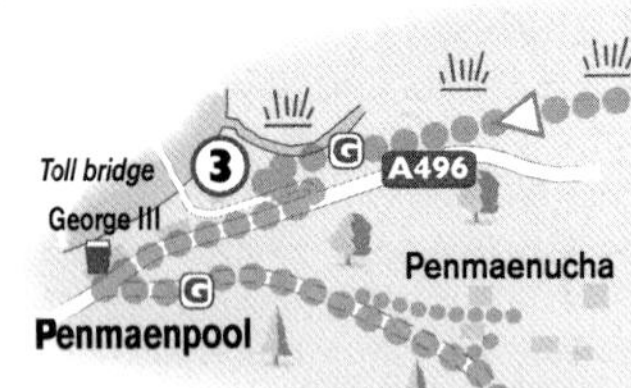

1 Walk through the car-park to the wall near the river Wnion. Turn LEFT and follow the Mawddach Trail alongside the river. *Look to the left and you'll see Mynydd Moel, the eastern peak of Cadair Idris, towering above Dolgellau.* When the track divides, bear RIGHT over a bridge. Then turn LEFT, for Penmaenpool, and continue alongside the river. Soon, walk through a gateway to a road. Cross this and turn RIGHT, then LEFT to re-join the Mawddach Trail.

2 Pass a car-park, then walk through a gateway and to the right of a cattle-grid. Continue on the trail which crosses two metal bridges. *You are now on the old railway line which linked Dolgellau with Penmaenpool and Barmouth. It opened in 1869, and closed in 1969.* Go alongside a locked gate and continue AHEAD on the trail, crossing a road. Soon go through a gateway into Penmaenpool car-park. *From here you can see the toll-bridge over the Mawddach river and the old railway signal-box.*

3 Go LEFT onto the road from the toll-bridge and follow it to the nearby A493. Go RIGHT and walk along the footpath on the right of the road. Ignore steps on the left and pass an entrance to the George

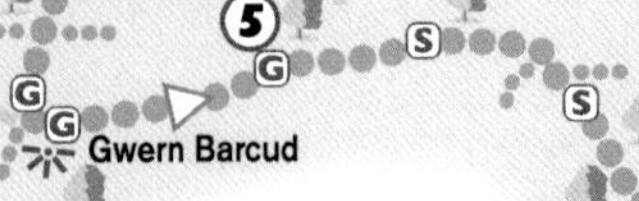

III Hotel. Then cross the road to a footpath sign and walk uphill on a path below a house. Ignore a path going right and continue to a footpath sign. Go up steps, through a metal gate and turn LEFT onto the track beyond. Follow this uphill and, when it

divides, bear RIGHT as indicated by the waymark. Continue alongside a wall (on the left), passing a gateway to Penmaenucha, the large house on your left. Pass another waymark, then steps to a bridge over the stream on your left. Then turn RIGHT at a waymark and follow a path uphill.

4 Soon go up some steps and over a wooden stile. *At the top of the slope beyond the stile look back for a good view of the Rhinog mountain peaks of (left to right) Diffwys, Y Lethr and Rhinog Fach.* Soon, turn RIGHT, as indicated, onto a track. Bear LEFT off the track, passing a wooden post and walking towards a waymark and yellow gate. Go through and bear to the LEFT of Gwern Barcud house, making for another waymark and metal gate. *The mountain ridge ahead of you here is Cadair Idris.* Go through and turn LEFT. Walk uphill across a field towards some trees on a hillock (on the right). Pass to the left of the trees and to the right of a second, higher, hillock. Then walk downhill towards a gate next to a wall which comes downhill on the left.

5 Go through the gate, ignoring the one on the right. Then bear HALF-RIGHT off the main track and walk downhill alongside the wall on your right. Ignore gates in the wall and, near a ruined barn, cross a stone stile next to a waymark. Turn RIGHT onto a track, then follow this LEFT past a waymark towards another waymark near a gate. Turn RIGHT at this waymark and cross a stream and wooden stile. Continue AHEAD past another waymark, then go to the RIGHT of a telegraph pole and walk HALF-RIGHT uphill towards a barn. Pass 40m to the LEFT of this and follow a rough path downhill to a track. Turn RIGHT onto this, then follow it LEFT uphill, passing a wooden gate.

6 Cross two streams then bear RIGHT at a waymark. Pass two more waymarks, then go RIGHT through a wooden gate. Turn RIGHT at the waymark just after it. Bear LEFT at the next waymark and pass a ruin (on the right). At the next waymark turn LEFT, cross a stream and continue uphill on a way-marked path to a road. *The house to your right as you walk is Llwyniarth.* Turn LEFT, ignoring a footpath sign pointing right, and follow the road. Go over two cattle-grids then past a footpath sign on the left. Continue on the road to a junction with a main road. Turn LEFT and follow this road downhill into Dolgellau. At a major junction, turn RIGHT, then LEFT onto a road going downhill. Follow this to Y Sospan restaurant. Turn RIGHT here for Eldon Square. For the Marian car-park turn LEFT, walk AHEAD then go RIGHT, then LEFT past Yr Hên Efail tea-rooms.

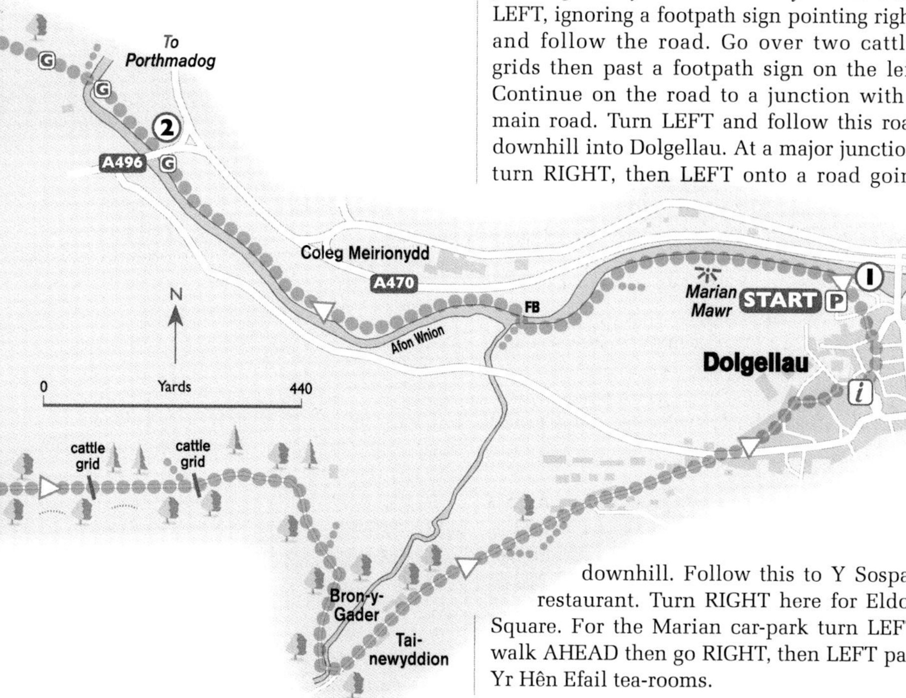

WALK 8

MARY'S WELL & A COMMUNITY GARDEN

DESCRIPTION An easy 1½-mile walk which takes you to several of Dolgellau's most interesting places. The walk is particularly suitable for children. Allow 1½ hours.

START Eldon Square bus-stop (SH728178). From the Marian car-park walk past Yr Hên Efail tea-rooms to a road. Turn RIGHT, then LEFT and pass Y Sospan restaurant. Go RIGHT, then LEFT to reach Eldon Square bus-stop.

DIRECTIONS Dolgellau can be reached from Porthmadog via the A487/A470, from Barmouth via the A496/A470, from Bala via the A494, from Machynlleth via the A487/A470, and from Tywyn via the A493. Park in the Marian Mawr car-park (SH 728179, post-code LL40 1UU) near the town-centre.

BUS SERVICES Buses 35 (from Blaenau Ffestiniog), 38 (from Barmouth), T2 (from Porthmadog and Machynlleth) and T3 (from Barmouth and Bala) serve Dolgellau. All buses stop in Eldon Square.

1 With your back to the bus-stop cross Eldon Square, turn RIGHT and walk AHEAD into Heol Feurig/Meyrick Street. Pass, on the right, Siop y Seren *(the upper storeys of which were used for weaving during the early 19th Century)* and then Dolgellau Catholic Church *(built in 1966)*. Pass Tan y Gader house *(once the town's maternity home)* and arrive at a cross-roads. *This is Y Domen Fawr, one of Dolgellau's smallest town squares.* Walk AHEAD onto a narrow road going uphill.

2 Pass Upperfield Street (on the right) and then take the next road on the right. *Pause near Bryn Teg house for a wonderful view over Dolgellau. You can see the church (see Walk 9) and Eldon Square.* Continue along the road to a junction. Ahead here is the impressive metal gateway to Ffynnon house, now a hotel.

3 Turn LEFT and walk uphill past Bryn Tirion house. Soon, go RIGHT at a footpath sign for Ffynnon Fair (Mary's Well) and follow a path past two wooden gates. Continue AHEAD, ignoring a path going uphill on the left. Soon you'll see a stone structure, with a metal gateway on the left. *This is Mary's Well which shares its dedication to St Mary with Dolgellau Church. It was believed that the water from the well had healing properties.* Continue on the path, walking to the left of a metal gate, to reach a wooden pig (on the left). *The sculpture commemorates the fact that this area of woodland was once grazed by pigs. It was commissioned from sculptor Nansi Hemming by the Dolgellau Partnership, which acquired and restored the well and woodland in 2006.*

4 Walk uphill to a wooden seat from where there is another good view over Dolgellau. *The mountain peak to the north is Y Garn, one of the Rhinog range.* Follow the path left up some wooden steps, ignoring another path going right to a kissing-gate and footpath sign. Continue AHEAD to another wooden kissing-gate. Go through and turn LEFT onto the road behind. *To the right of the track opposite is the gateway to Coed Ffridd Jêl, National Park woodland open to the public.* Continue along the road to its end near Pen y Banc house.

5 Go LEFT near a bridleway sign and downhill to a seat. *This is another spectacular viewpoint. The high, rounded hill above Dolgellau is Moel Offrwm, an ancient hill-fort.* Go RIGHT at the footpath sign and downhill to a bridleway sign and road. Cross this and bear LEFT downhill past Hafod house. Turn RIGHT at a footpath sign, walk downhill and cross a footbridge over the Aran river. *The source of the Aran is high on Cadair Idris mountain.* Walk through a gate to a road and footpath sign. Go RIGHT then cross the road to Felin Uchaf, Dolgellau's community garden. *This is open to the public.*

6 Turn RIGHT after leaving the garden and walk downhill. Continue AHEAD alongside the Aran at a junction. When this road bears right continue beside the river to Aran

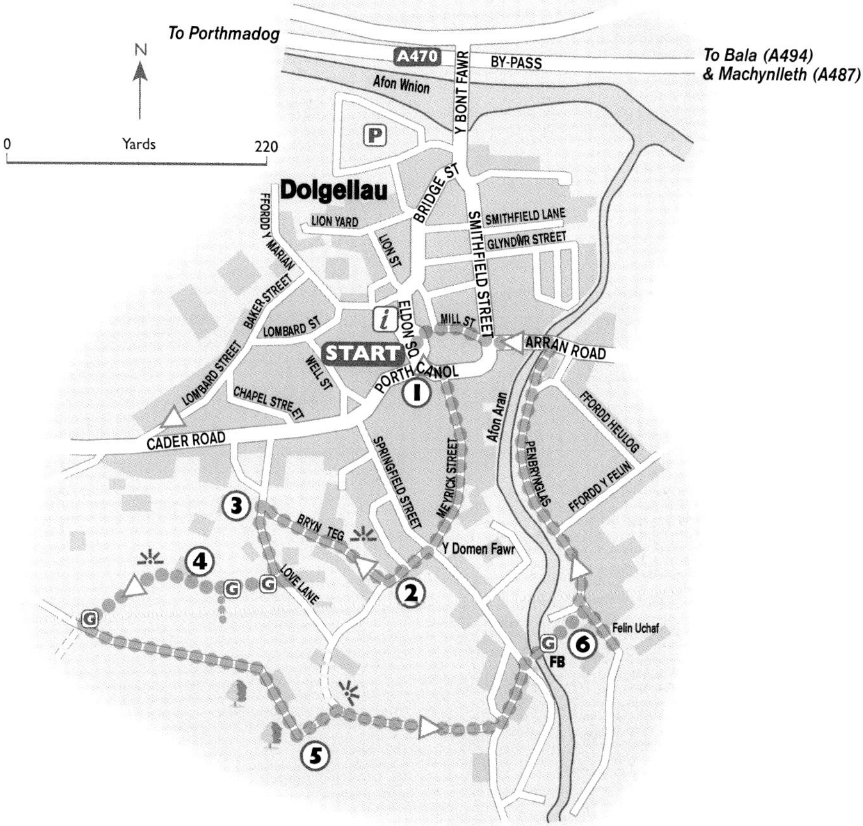

To Porthmadog
N
0 Yards 220
A470
BY-PASS
To Bala (A494) & Machynlleth (A487)
Afon Wnion
Y BONT FAWR
P
Dolgellau
BRIDGE ST
FFORDD Y MARIAN
LION YARD
LION ST
SMITHFIELD LANE
GLYNDŴR STREET
SMITHFIELD STREET
BAKER STREET
LOMBARD ST
ELDON SQ
MILL ST
START
ARRAN ROAD
LOMBARD STREET
WELL ST
PORTH CANOL
CHAPEL STREET
CADER ROAD
Afon Aran
FFORDD HEULOG
SPRINGFIELD STREET
MEYRICK STREET
PENBRYNGLAS
FFORDD Y FELIN
BRYN TEG
Y Domen Fawr
LOVE LANE
Felin Uchaf
FB
1 2 3 4 5 6

Bridge. *Two centuries ago this area was at the centre of Dolgellau's woollen industry.* Walk LEFT to Y Meirionnydd hotel and cross the road into Mill Street. Walk past the Cross Keys pub and turn LEFT into Eldon Square.

St Mary's Well

WALK 9

DOLGELLAU'S CHURCH & TWO RIVERS

DESCRIPTION An easy 1½-mile walk which helps to set Dolgellau in its historical and geographical context. The walk is particularly suitable for children. Allow 1½ hours.

START Eldon Square bus-stop (SH728178). From the Marian car-park walk past Yr Hên Efail tea-rooms to a road. Turn RIGHT, then LEFT and pass Y Sospan restaurant. Go RIGHT, then LEFT to reach Eldon Square bus-stop.

DIRECTIONS Dolgellau can be reached from Porthmadog via the A487/A470, from Barmouth via the A496/A470, from Bala via the A494, from Machynlleth via the A487/A470, and from Tywyn via the A493. Park in the Marian Mawr car-park (SH 728179, post-code LL40 1UU) near the town-centre.

BUS SERVICES Buses 35 (from Blaenau Ffestiniog), 38 (from Barmouth), T2 (from Porthmadog and Machynlleth) and T3 (from Barmouth and Bala) serve Dolgellau. All buses stop in Eldon Square.

1 With your back to the bus-stop turn RIGHT then go RIGHT through an arcade. Turn RIGHT down steps and RIGHT again to Plas Brith. Go RIGHT, then LEFT into Ffordd y Marian and RIGHT to Dolgellau church, St Mary's. *The first reference to a church here was in 1254. The present building dates from about 1716.* Return to Marian Road and turn RIGHT.

2 Cross the road to a metal gate and graveyard. Walkthrough the gate, then RIGHT to an unusual pyramid-like monument. *This is dedicated to a local schoolmaster and bard Dafydd Ionawr.* Return to the road, turn LEFT and walk to the Marian Mawr. *This green space was donated to the town in 1811. The stone circle (on the left) was created for the 1949 National Eisteddfod.*

3 Walk AHEAD across the grass to a raised bank. *Beyond the bank is Dolgellau's main river, the Wnion. There is an excellent view from here back over Dolgellau to Mynydd Moel, the easternmost peak of Cadair Idris.* Turn RIGHT by the river, passing a Mawddach Trail notice-board (see Walk 7). Continue to Y Bont Fawr, the bridge over the Wnion.

4 Cross the road at the bridge-end and pass the old County Hall. *This dates from 1825 and is still used as a courthouse.* Go through a gate into a park then HALF-LEFT. *Here there's a railway truck from a gold mine and a wooden sculpture by Alan Mantle entitled Roots.* Continue alongside the river, then walk RIGHT past Dolgellau's war memorial. *Behind the memorial is an exercise area for adults and children over 12.* Walk LEFT through a gate and past a children's playground. Cross a footbridge over the Aran river and pass the Glan Wnion Leisure Centre. *The Aran's source is high on Cadair Idris. It flows into the Wnion nearby and was once heavily industrialised with fulling mills and tanning yards.*

5 Turn RIGHT across the Co-op car-park. Then bear RIGHT and walk to Aran Bridge. *Two centuries ago this area was at the centre of Dolgellau's woollen industry.* Cross the main road and continue alongside the river. Bear RIGHT onto a road. At a junction go AHEAD then RIGHT at a footpath sign. Walk through a gate and cross another footbridge over the Aran. Walk uphill then RIGHT. Go RIGHT at a road junction and downhill.

6 Soon you will arrive at a crossroads. *This is Y Domen fawr, one of Dolgellau's smallest town squares.* From here continue AHEAD along Heol Plas Uchaf/Springfield Street. Turn LEFT, passing a telephone box. Cross the road by Rhug house and follow a road RIGHT past a chapel. Go RIGHT to a junction and then RIGHT into Y Lawnt/ Lombard Street. *The building with arched windows here is Dolgellau's former police station. It was built in the mid-19thC.*

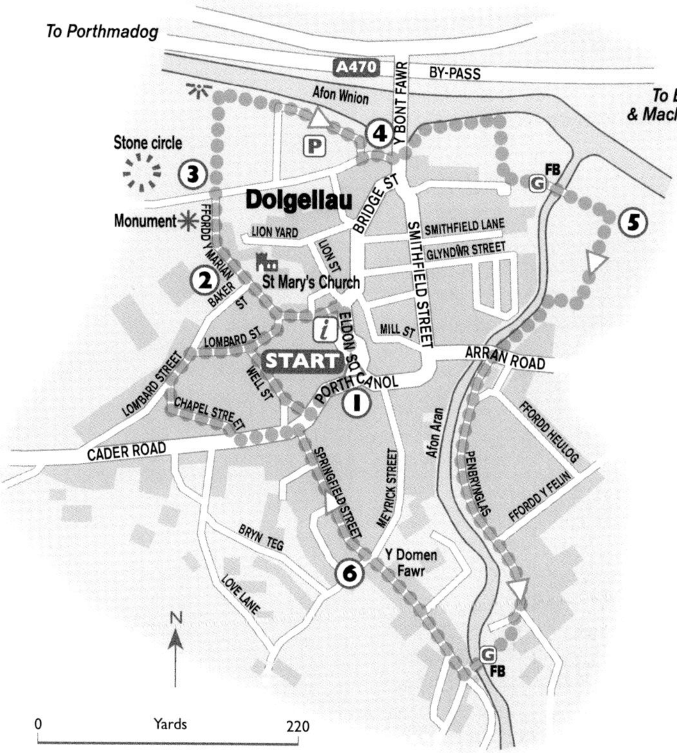

Follow Lombard Street to Y Sospan restaurant *(Dolgellau's original courthouse).* Here, go RIGHT to Eldon Square or LEFT to the Marian Car-park.

Dafydd Ionawr Monument and Dolgellau Church

WALK 10

N FARM & LLWYNIARTH

DESCRIPTION A 4-mile walk which uses woodland paths to take you high above the Mawddach Valley. You'll cross rushing streams and climb through secluded meadows to arrive at a viewpoint from where the peaks of northern Snowdonia can be seen. (Please note a short section of Stage 2 of Walk 10 involves walking along a main road without pavements). Allow 3½ hours.

START Marian Mawr car-park near Dolgellau town-centre (SH 728179). From Eldon Square bus-stop turn LEFT (with your back to the bus-stop) and walk to Lombard Street. Turn RIGHT, then LEFT, past Y Sospan restaurant. Continue AHEAD, then go RIGHT, then LEFT down an alley-way past Yr Hên Efail tea-rooms.

DIRECTIONS Dolgellau can be reached from Porthmadog via the A487/A470, from Barmouth via the A496/A470, from Bala via the A494, from Machynlleth via the A487/A470, and from Tywyn via the A493. Park in the Marian Mawr car-park (SH 728179, post-code LL40 1UU) near the town-centre.

BUS SERVICES Buses 35 (from Blaenau Ffestiniog), 38 (from Barmouth), T2 (from Porthmadog and Machynlleth) and T3 (from Barmouth and Bala) serve Dolgellau. All buses stop in Eldon Square.

1 Walk through the car-park towards the river Wnion. Turn LEFT and follow the Mawddach Trail alongside the river. *Look to the left for a good view of Mynydd Moel, the eastern peak of Cadair Idris, which towers above Dolgellau.* When the track divides, bear RIGHT across a bridge over the river. Then turn LEFT for Penmaenpool and, soon, walk through a gateway to a road.

2 Turn LEFT and walk across the Wnion on a road bridge. Turn LEFT, walking alongside a crash barrier on the left verge of a road signposted for Dolgellau. Cross the road at the 'Welcome to Dolgellau' sign. Turn LEFT, and walk along the right-hand side of the road. Soon, go RIGHT near a post-box and uphill on a minor road. *Before long there are views over the upper Mawddach Valley to Llanelltyd (see Walk 16).* Pass the entrance to Bryn Adda house (on the left) and continue AHEAD through a gateway.

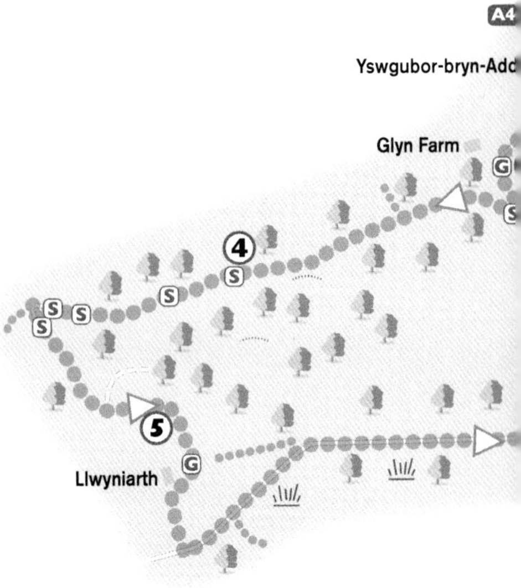

3 Near Glyn Farm turn LEFT at a footpath sign and go through a metal gate. Follow a track then, when it bears left, continue AHEAD on the left of a water course and a wall. Near where the wall bears left, cross over it using a high stone stile. Go RIGHT to follow the path beyond, which is initially parallel with the wall. Pass farm buildings (below, on the right) then bear LEFT at a yellow waymark. Follow the winding path uphill through a gully, passing a metal water container then two more waymarks. Ignore gaps in the wall on your left, then follow the path downhill through trees. Go LEFT through the wall, where there are waymarks, and turn RIGHT through a, old gateway. Follow the path as it bears LEFT and goes downhill.

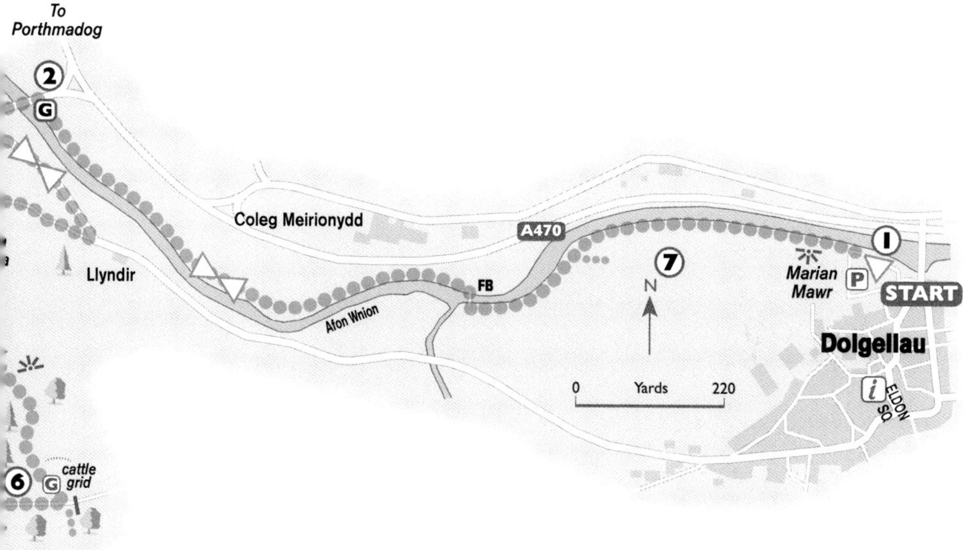

4 Cross a stream to a wooden gate and waymark. Go over the stile to the left of the gate and bear LEFT, alongside a fence, to another stile and waymark. Walk AHEAD alongside a low wall, then go HALF-RIGHT uphill through trees. Bear LEFT past a waymark, ignoring a metal gate ahead. Climb over a stone stile in the wall, then walk AHEAD across a field towards a waymark and stile on the left of a gate. Cross the stile and a stream, then go LEFT at a waymark onto a path which crosses another stream and stile. Continue AHEAD past another waymark, then go to the RIGHT of a telegraph pole and walk HALF-RIGHT uphill towards a barn. Pass about 40m to the left of this and follow a rough path downhill to a track. Turn RIGHT onto this, then follow it LEFT uphill, passing a wooden gate.

5 Cross two streams then bear RIGHT at a waymark. Pass two more waymarks, then go RIGHT through a wooden gate. Turn RIGHT at the waymark just after it. Bear LEFT at the next waymark and pass a ruined building (on the right). At the next marker turn LEFT, cross a stream and continue AHEAD uphill on a way-marked path to a road. *The house to your right as walk you is Llwyniarth.* Turn LEFT onto the road. *There are good views of northern Snowdonia from here.* Ignore a footpath sign pointing right and follow the road over a cattle-grid. Turn LEFT at a footpath sign just before a second cattle-grid.

6 Go through a wooden gate and downhill on a path to the right of a fence and trees. Soon, cross a stream. *Below you, to the right, you can see Bryn Adda house and, ahead, Glyn Farm. The mountain in the distance beyond the farm is Diffwys, a peak in the Rhinog range.* Go through a metal gate and continue AHEAD, with a high wall on your left, towards the Glyn Farm buildings. Bear RIGHT near the stone stile you crossed earlier and walk downhill alongside the water course. Join a track coming in from the right. Pass a footpath sign and go through a metal gate. Turn RIGHT and retrace your steps back to Eldon Square. *Please note that, when you arrive back at the post-box and main road, you should cross the road and turn LEFT to walk on the right-hand side of the road back to the Mawddach Trail.*

WALK 11

TAN Y FEDW & GWERNAN LAKE

DESCRIPTION A 4½-mile walk which takes you up into the foothills of Cadair Idris. The walk provides wonderful views over Dolgellau and the upper Mawddach estuary, and skirts Llyn Gwernan, a lake in the most spectacular of settings. Allow 4½ hours.

START Eldon Square bus-stop (SH 728178). From the Marian car-park walk past Yr Hên Efail tea-rooms to a road. Turn RIGHT, then LEFT and pass Y Sospan restaurant. Go RIGHT, then LEFT to reach Eldon Square bus-stop.

DIRECTIONS Dolgellau can be reached from Porthmadog via the A487/A470, from Barmouth via the A496/A470, from Bala via the A494, from Machynlleth via the A487/A470, and from Tywyn via the A493. Park in the Marian Mawr car-park (SH 728179, post-code LL40 1UU) near the town-centre.

BUS SERVICES Buses 35 (from Blaenau Ffestiniog), 38 (from Barmouth), T2 (from Porthmadog and Machynlleth) and T3 (from Barmouth and Bala) serve Dolgellau. All buses stop in Eldon Square

1 With your back to the bus-stop turn RIGHT then go RIGHT through an arcade. Take the first road on the LEFT (Heol Plas Uchaf/Springfield Street) and follow this uphill. Continue AHEAD at a cross-roads, ignore a road going left and, when the road divides, go to the RIGHT. Soon turn RIGHT at a bridleway sign and walk uphill. Turn LEFT at a footpath sign and continue to a road.

2 Turn LEFT at a bridleway sign. At a junction go RIGHT (following the bridleway) and continue uphill. Go through a metal gate and follow a grassy track RIGHT, then, after a short distance, LEFT across a stream. *Soon, there is a good view of the eastern summit of Cadair Idris ahead.* The track, now stony, descends (ignore a minor track going right) and then continues alongside a stream. Go through a metal gate and cross a road to a bridleway sign. Follow the path beyond, walking HALF-RIGHT across rough ground.

3 Pass a waymark and cross a bridge over a stream. Walk uphill, making for another waymark. The next waymark points left; ignore this and continue AHEAD here, passing another waymark. Soon, cross a wooden stile over a wall. Walk alongside the wall to a gate and another stile, alongside a waymark. Go over and walk beside a wall on your left. Look for a waymark AHEAD by a gap in a wall. Go through, turn RIGHT and then bear RIGHT again to walk to the right of a ruined house. *This is Tan y Fedw, a settlement sheltered by Cadair Idris and with views of the Rhinog mountains to the north.*

4 Continue past the house and bear RIGHT onto a track coming from the left. Go over a stile alongside a metal gate and continue towards a house. Go through a wooden gate with waymark, then to the left of a barn and through a metal gate. Continue uphill alongside a wall towards another house. Walk through a metal gate, cross a stream, then go over

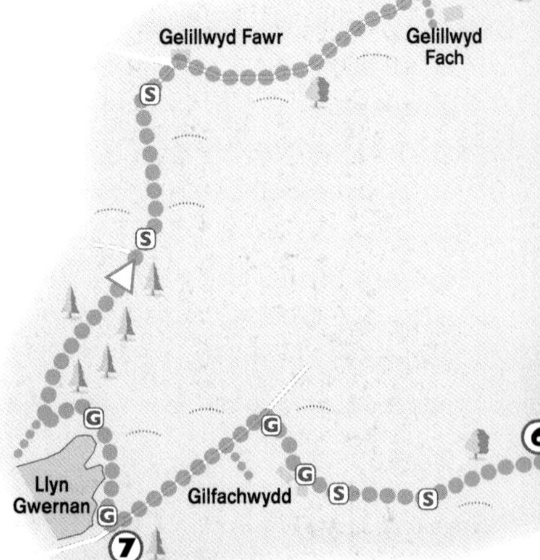

a stile adjoining another metal gate. Pass Brynrhug and go RIGHT past a waymark and Hendy house. When the track goes right, continue AHEAD past another waymark, through a metal gate and across a stream. *(If this is in flood return to the track and follow it LEFT to a road. Turn LEFT then*

LEFT again, and walk to the entrance to Llyn Gwernan. Resume the walk at Stage 7).

5 Ignore a path going right just after the stream and continue AHEAD then through a metal gate next to a footpath sign. Bear HALF-RIGHT, making for another metal gate and waymarks. Go through and AHEAD, passing Tan y Gader farm. Go through another metal gate with waymarks and past a barn. Then bear HALF-LEFT to a gateway and waymark. Cross a stream and walk AHEAD towards another gate and waymark. *There is a good view to the right from here of four of the Rhinog mountain peaks (from left to right): Diffwys, Y Lethr, Rhinog Fach and Y Garn.*

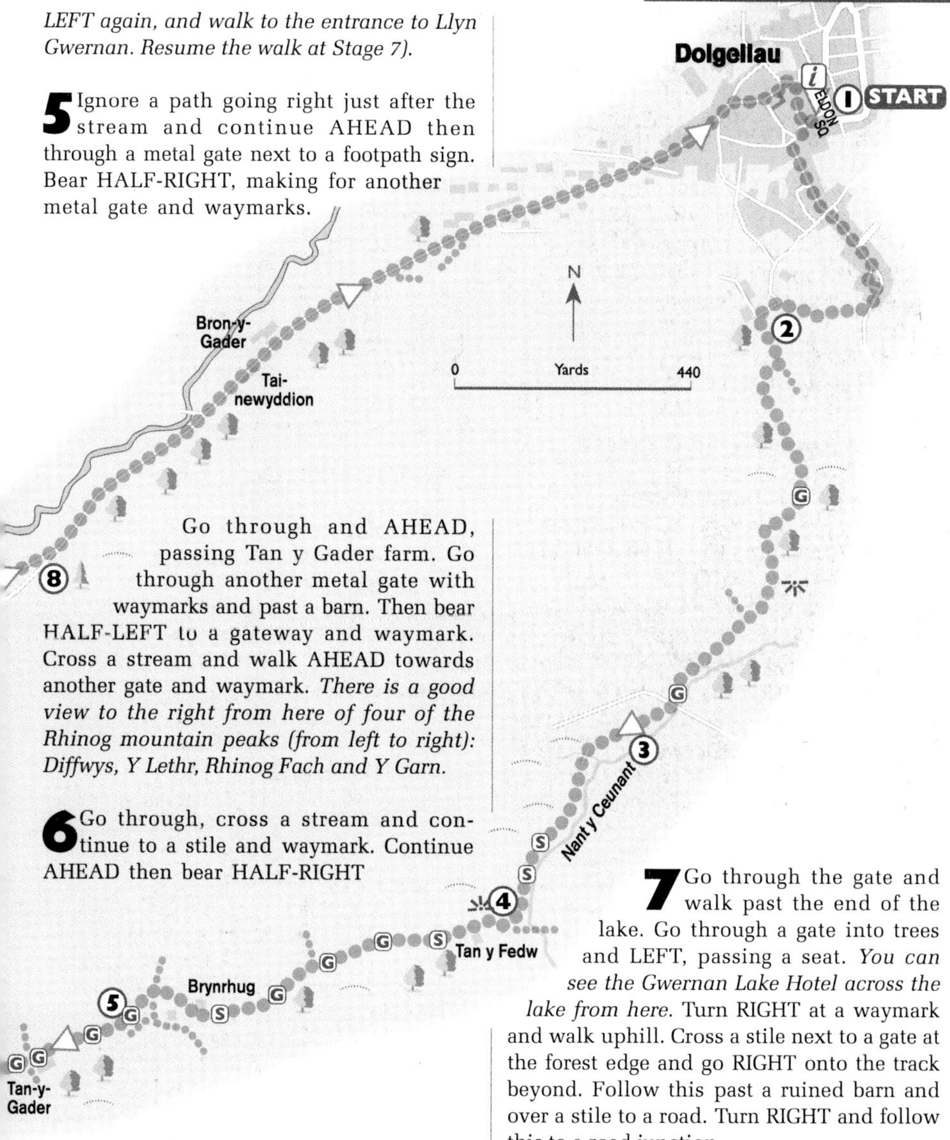

6 Go through, cross a stream and continue to a stile and waymark. Continue AHEAD then bear HALF-RIGHT towards a house. Cross a stile next to a waymark and bear HALF-RIGHT alongside a fence and the house (Gilfachwydd). Pass a waymark and go RIGHT down steps and through a wooden gate. Turn RIGHT onto a track, pass a waymark and go through a gate to a road. Go LEFT onto the road. Ignore a path going left and continue to a metal gate and Llyn Gwernan sign (on the right).

7 Go through the gate and walk past the end of the lake. Go through a gate into trees and LEFT, passing a seat. *You can see the Gwernan Lake Hotel across the lake from here.* Turn RIGHT at a waymark and walk uphill. Cross a stile next to a gate at the forest edge and go RIGHT onto the track beyond. Follow this past a ruined barn and over a stile to a road. Turn RIGHT and follow this to a road junction.

8 Turn LEFT and follow the road you've joined downhill into Dolgellau. At a main road junction, turn RIGHT then go LEFT onto a road going downhill. Follow this road, Y Lawnt/Lombard Street, until you reach Y Sospan restaurant (on the left). From here go RIGHT to Eldon Square bus-stop and LEFT to the Marian Car-park.

WALK 12

TABOR & THE QUAKERS

DESCRIPTION This 4½-mile walk follows a track above the Aran river to Plas y Brithdir farm. It continues across meadows and through woodland to the old Quaker meeting house at Tabor. The return to Dolgellau uses a series of old paths linking houses and mills on the slopes of Cadair Idris. Allow 4 hours.

START Eldon Square bus-stop (SH 728178). From the Marian car-park walk past Yr Hên Efail tea-rooms to a road. Turn RIGHT, then LEFT and pass Y Sospan restaurant. Go RIGHT, then LEFT to reach Eldon Square bus-stop.

DIRECTIONS Dolgellau can be reached from Porthmadog via the A487/A470, from Barmouth via the A496/A470, from Bala via the A494, from Machynlleth via the A487/A470, and from Tywyn via the A493. Park in the Marian Mawr car-park (SH 728179, post-code LL40 1UU) near the town-centre.

BUS SERVICES Buses 35 (from Blaenau Ffestiniog), 38 (from Barmouth), T2 (from Porthmadog and Machynlleth) and T3 (from Barmouth and Bala) serve Dolgellau. All buses stop in Eldon Square.

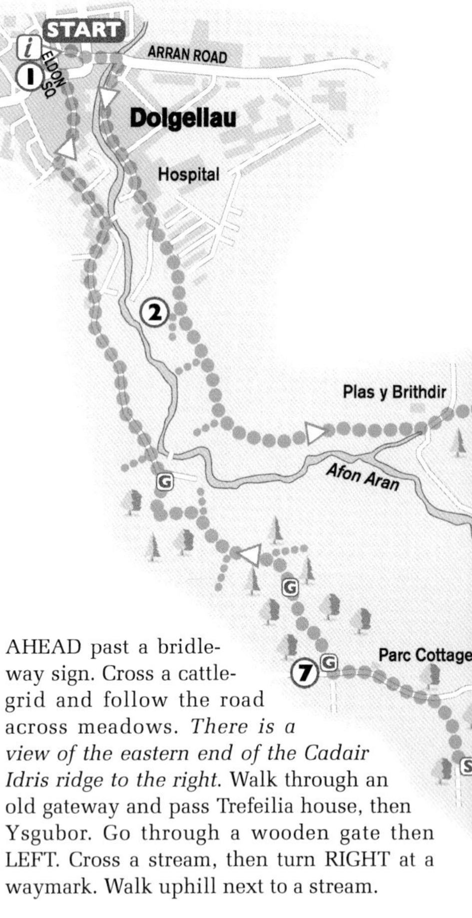

1 Cross Eldon Square to the HSBC Bank. Turn LEFT, then RIGHT, and RIGHT again opposite the Cross Keys pub. Follow Mill Street to a junction. Cross the road towards Y Meirionnydd hotel and turn LEFT. Cross the Aran Bridge. *Two centuries ago this area was at the centre of Dolgellau's woollen industry.* Walk RIGHT alongside the river. Go RIGHT onto a road. At a junction continue AHEAD, passing footpath signs to right and left. Continue uphill.

2 Soon the road becomes a track. Pass three entrances to Coed Aberneint on the right (see Walks 1 and 6). *The Aran river flows through the gorge below you in Coed Aberneint. Its source is high on the slopes of Cadair Idris.* Pass Frongoch house before reaching a road. Go AHEAD past Plas y Brithdir farm (on the left). At a junction walk AHEAD past a bridleway sign. Cross a cattle-grid and follow the road across meadows. *There is a view of the eastern end of the Cadair Idris ridge to the right.* Walk through an old gateway and pass Trefeilia house, then Ysgubor. Go through a wooden gate then LEFT. Cross a stream, then turn RIGHT at a waymark. Walk uphill next to a stream.

3 Cross a stile alongside a wooden gate and continue uphill. Pass some telegraph poles and a waymark, then a gate (on the right). Soon, go RIGHT over a wooden stile then LEFT uphill past a footpath sign to a track. Turn LEFT and pass Coed Ceunant house. Soon, cross a cattle-grid and bear LEFT at the entrance to Hafodlas caravan park. Ignore a track going left then turn RIGHT onto a road opposite a bridleway sign. Walk uphill past Groeslwyd and then Fronoleu hotel. Ignore a footpath sign pointing right and continue on the road until you reach a junction near a post-box and Tabor Chapel. *The chapel was once a Quaker meeting house. Quakers from the Dolgellau area emigrated to America after persecution during the 17thC.*

4 Turn RIGHT at the junction, pass an information board and go through a metal gate. Turn RIGHT and follow a track to another noticeboard. *Beyond this are the ruins of Dewisbren Uchaf, once the home of Dorothy Owen, a famous Quaker preacher.* Continue uphill, ignoring a footpath sign indicating left. *To the right there is a spectacular view of the Mawddach Estuary and Rhinog mountains.* Continue downhill on the track and through a wooden gate. Soon go RIGHT through a wall, then follow a track LEFT downhill to a footpath sign alongside Dref Gerrig house.

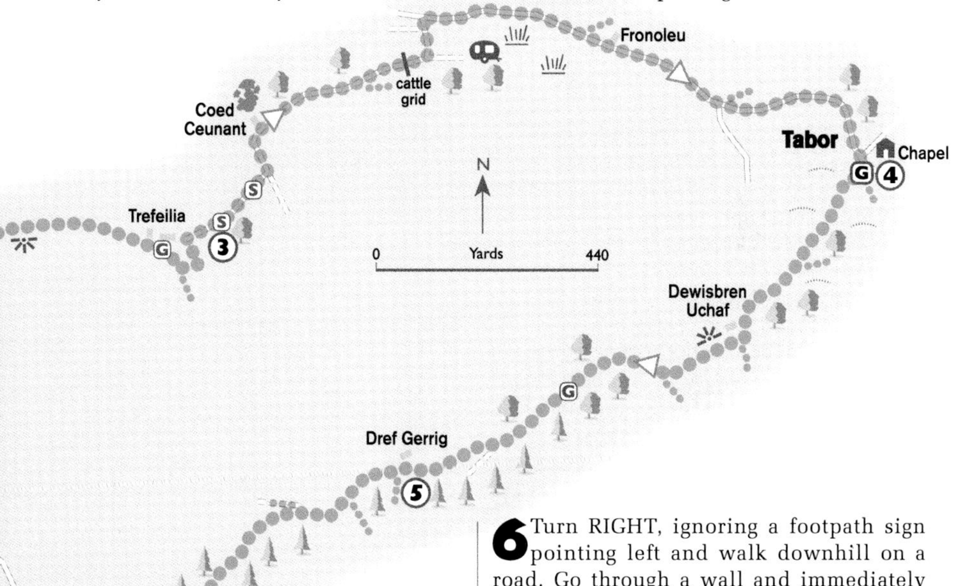

5 Continue on a road, ignoring a footpath sign pointing left. Cross a stream and go LEFT at a second footpath sign. Follow a path through trees, across a stream, then through a wall and past a ruined barn. *From here there is a good view, ahead, of the eastern summit of Cadair Idris.* Cross more streams and then a clearing (*for a gas-pipe line*) to reach a road and footpath sign. Turn LEFT, past a house, then RIGHT through a metal gate. Walk downhill, past Pandy Gader house. Go HALF-RIGHT, through a gate and over a footbridge (*across the Aran again*) to a footpath sign.

6 Turn RIGHT, ignoring a footpath sign pointing left and walk downhill on a road. Go through a wall and immediately LEFT at a waymark. Cross a stile and walk AHEAD on a path. Bear HALF-RIGHT, pass a waymark and walk alongside a wall. Pass another waymark and go downhill to a stile. Go over and down steps past a waymark. Turn RIGHT and follow a track downhill to a road and footpath sign. Turn LEFT and walk past Parc Cottage to a gateway and footpath sign on the right.

7 Go RIGHT and follow a track past two waymarks. Soon bear RIGHT where a track goes left through a gate and continue to a wooden gate. Go through and downhill to a junction of paths. Turn LEFT onto a wider path, then ignore a path going left. Ignore a path going right and continue downhill, following the main path RIGHT before going past a footpath sign and through a gateway to a road. Turn LEFT here and follow the road uphill. Pass Argraig house, ignore a footpath sign, then a bridleway sign, pointing left and pass a minor road going right. At a crossroads turn RIGHT and follow Meyrick Street/Heol Feurig back to Eldon Square.

WALK 13

GRAIG & LLWYNIARTH

DESCRIPTION This 4½-mile walk takes you into the foothills of Cadair Idris to the west of Dolgellau. On the way you'll pass some beautifully situated settlements and visit viewpoints from where the summits of mountains in northern Snowdonia can be seen. Allow four hours.

START Eldon Square bus-stop (SH 728178). From the Marian car-park walk past Yr Hên Efail tea-rooms to a road. Turn RIGHT, then LEFT and pass Y Sospan restaurant. Go RIGHT, then LEFT to reach Eldon Square bus-stop.

DIRECTIONS Dolgellau can be reached from Porthmadog via the A487/A470, from Barmouth via the A496/A470, from Bala via the A494, from Machynlleth via the A487/A470, and from Tywyn via the A493. Park in the Marian Mawr car-park (SH 728179, post-code LL40 1UU) near the town-centre.

BUS SERVICES Buses 35 (from Blaenau Ffestiniog), 38 (from Barmouth), T2 (from Porthmadog and Machynlleth) and T3 (from Barmouth and Bala) serve Dolgellau. All buses stop in Eldon Square.

1 With your back to the bus-stop, cross Eldon Square, turn RIGHT, cross the road ahead and walk into Heol Feurig/Meyrick Street. Pass Siop y Seren and a chapel (on the right) and then the Catholic Church (on the left). *The upper floors of Siop y Seren were used for weaving during the 19thC and the Catholic Church was opened in 1966.* Continue AHEAD to a junction. Walk AHEAD, crossing Springfield Street/ Heol Plas Uchaf to join a narrow road going uphill. Pass Upperfield Street then Bryn Teg (both on the right) and continue AHEAD steeply uphill to a junction. Go RIGHT and downhill.

2 Turn LEFT at a waymark for Ffynnon Fair (Mary's Well) and follow a path to the left of a wooden gate. Then walk a short distance on a track between walls to another wooden gate. Pass this on the left and continue AHEAD, ignoring a path going uphill on the left alongside a fence. Soon you'll see a stone structure, with a metal gateway on the left. *This is Mary's Well, which shares its dedication to St Mary with Dolgellau Church. Roman coins were found nearby during the 17thC.* Continue on the path, walking to the left of a metal gate, to reach a wooden pig (on the left). *Fifty years ago this area of woodland was grazed by pigs. The wooden pig commemorates this fact. It was commissioned from sculptor Nansi Hemming by the Dolgellau Partnership when they bought and improved the area for the local community.*

3 Walk uphill to a wooden seat from where there is a good view over Dolgellau. *The mountain to the north of the town is Y Garn, one of the Rhinog range.* Follow the path LEFT up some wooden steps, then go RIGHT through a kissing-gate to a road. Turn RIGHT and follow the road past a footpath sign (on the right) to a junction. Go LEFT and walk uphill on this road for some distance. Pass the last houses (on the left), then a road going right and the entrance to Waen Hir. Take the next RIGHT (sign-posted Tal y Waen) and follow this road to a waymark and entrance to Graig. Go through the metal

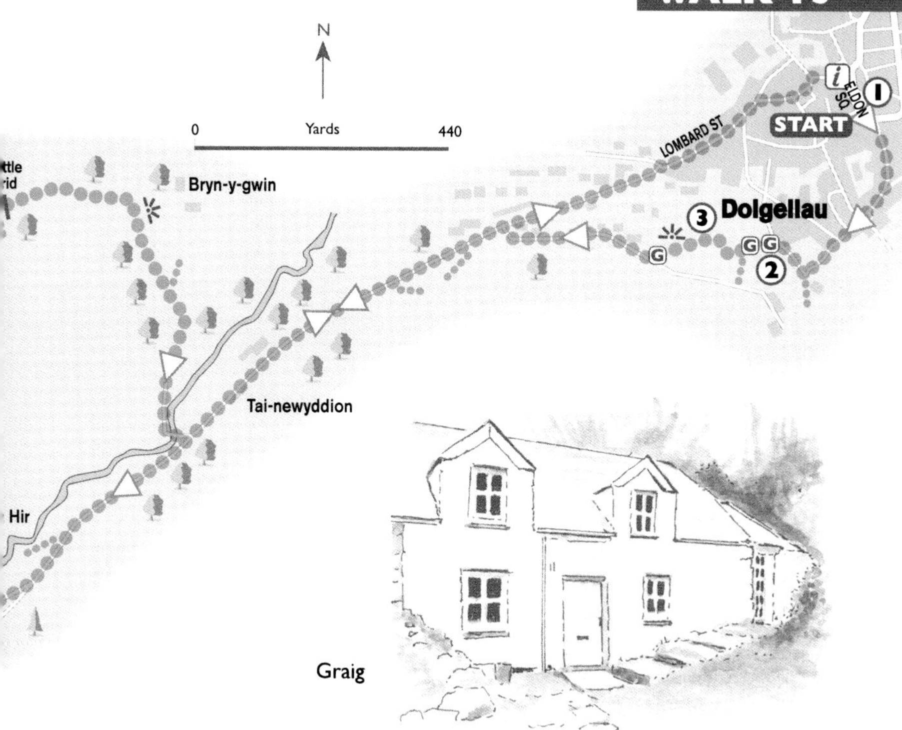

gate and follow the track across a stream and uphill to the house. *There are magnificent views of the summit of Cadair Idris (to the left) just before Graig.* Turn LEFT at a waymark just before the building and follow a path to a way-marked junction.

4 Walk RIGHT uphill, passing a waymark and going through a gully. Ignore a path going right. Pass another waymark as you follow the path through trees. Bear RIGHT uphill and continue alongside a wall on the right. Soon the path leaves the wall and descends to another waymark. It then follows a short stone gully before going downhill to another waymark, where another path comes in from the left. *There are more views of Cadair Idris from here.* Continue AHEAD uphill then bear LEFT towards a gate and stile. Go through/over, ignoring a faint path going right, to another waymark. *From here you can see Diffwys (ahead) and Y Garn (on the right). These mountains also belong to the Rhinog range.* Go RIGHT to another waymark. Then bear RIGHT downhill, keeping to the main path, which goes through bushes and some muddy patches to another waymark. Bear LEFT and make for a footpath sign alongside a road.

5 Turn RIGHT onto the road and follow it a short distance uphill. *There are wonderful views to the left from here. The house below you is Llwyniarth and northwards you can see the upper Mawddach Valley, Coed y Brenin, the Rhinog mountains and Snowdon itself.* Continue on the road, crossing two cattle-grids and ignoring a footpath sign pointing left. The road descends, turns RIGHT *(at which point there's a good view of Dolgellau)* and then reaches a junction. Turn LEFT and follow this road downhill into Dolgellau, ignoring the road (on the right) which you used earlier. At a junction with a main road cross this road, turn RIGHT then go LEFT downhill. Follow this road, Y Lawnt/Lombard Street, until you reach Y Sospan restaurant (on the left). From here go RIGHT to Eldon Square bus-stop or LEFT to the Marian car-park

WALK 14

RHYDWEN & GLYN FARM

DESCRIPTION A 4½-mile walk which takes you to some remote settlements and spectacular viewpoints above Dolgellau to the south. (Please note a short section of Stage 8 of Walk 14 involves walking along a main road without pavements). Allow 4½ hours.

START Eldon Square bus-stop (SH 728178). From the Marian car-park walk past Yr Hên Efail tea-rooms to a road. Turn RIGHT, then LEFT and pass Y Sospan restaurant. Go RIGHT, then LEFT to reach Eldon Square bus-stop.

DIRECTIONS Dolgellau can be reached from Porthmadog via the A487/A470, from Barmouth via the A496/A470, from Bala via the A494, from Machynlleth via the A487/A470, and from Tywyn via the A493. Park in the Marian Mawr car-park (SH 728179, post-code LL40 1UU) near the town-centre.

BUS SERVICES Buses 35 (from Blaenau Ffestiniog), 38 (from Barmouth), T2 (from Porthmadog and Machynlleth) and T3 (from Barmouth and Bala) serve Dolgellau. All buses stop in Eldon Square.

1 With your back to the bus-stop turn RIGHT then go RIGHT through an arcade. Cross the road and take the first LEFT (Heol Plas Uchaf/Springfield Street). Turn RIGHT into Upperfield Street, then go RIGHT at a junction and uphill. Ignore a right turn then, when the road bears right, go AHEAD past Pen y Bryn house. At a footpath sign go RIGHT uphill to a road and bridleway sign.

2 Go LEFT uphill, then RIGHT, as indicated by the bridleway sign. Go through a gate and follow a track RIGHT, then LEFT across a stream. The track descends (ignore a minor track going right), continuing alongside a stream. Go through a gate and RIGHT onto a road opposite a bridleway sign. Soon, go through a metal gate. Pass the entrance to Brynrhug and bear RIGHT past a house. *From here there is a view of the Rhinog mountains to the north.* Continue past Rhydwen house to a junction.

3 Go RIGHT then LEFT to a footpath sign. Walk over a slate stile and across a field.

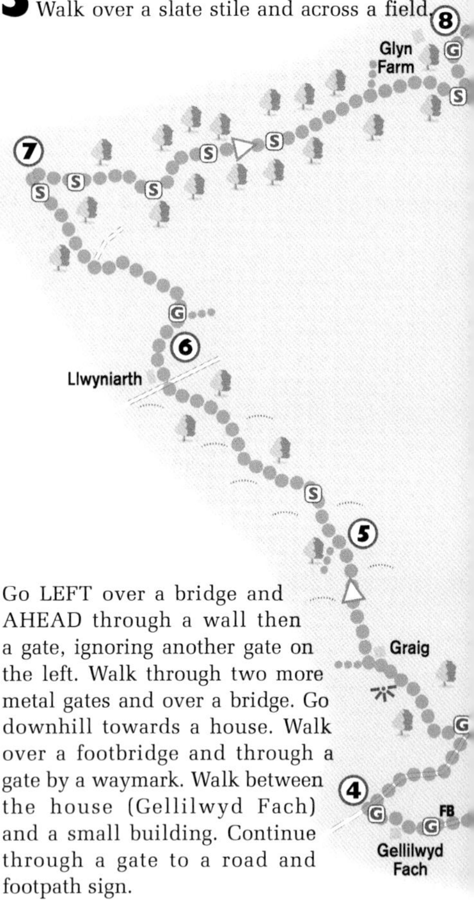

Go LEFT over a bridge and AHEAD through a wall then a gate, ignoring another gate on the left. Walk through two more metal gates and over a bridge. Go downhill towards a house. Walk over a footbridge and through a gate by a waymark. Walk between the house (Gellilwyd Fach) and a small building. Continue through a gate to a road and footpath sign.

4 Walk RIGHT downhill to a footpath sign by a gate marked Graig (on the left). Go through, over a bridge and uphill to Graig. *There are magnificent views of the summit of Cadair Idris (to the left) just before Graig.* Turn LEFT at a waymark just before the building and RIGHT at a way-marked junction. Walk uphill, passing a waymark, and through a gully. Ignore a path going right. Pass another waymark as you walk through trees. Bear RIGHT uphill and continue alongside a wall. Soon the path leaves the wall and descends to another waymark. It then follows a short stone gully before going downhill to another waymark. Ignore the path coming in on the the left.

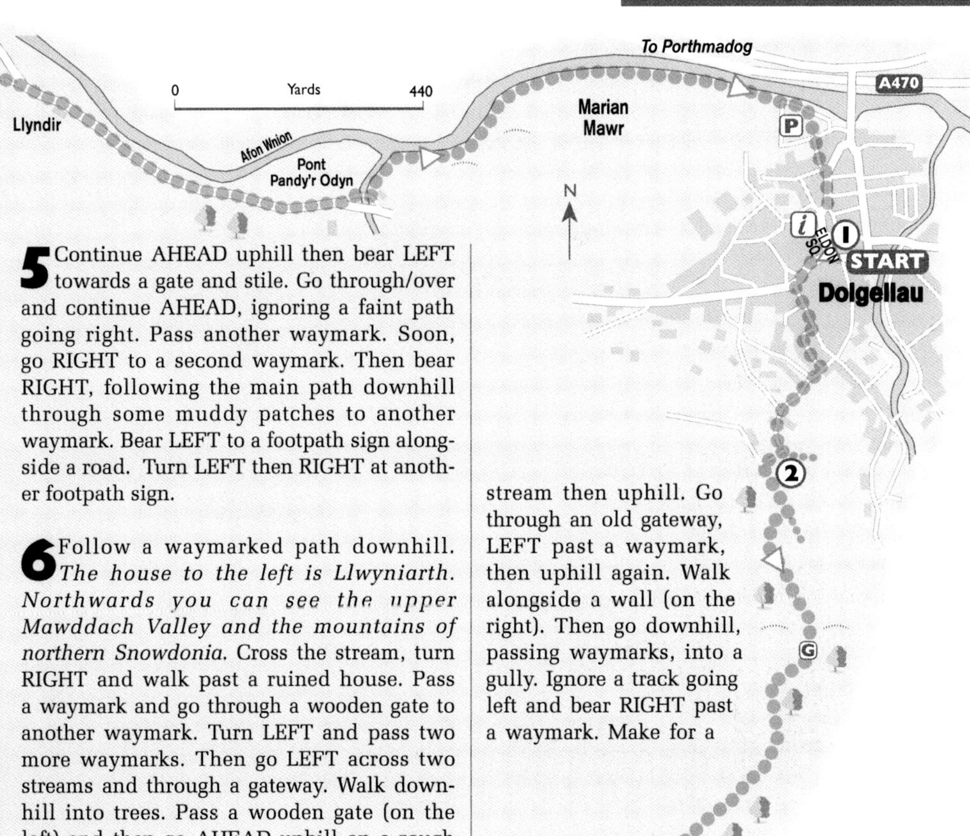

5 Continue AHEAD uphill then bear LEFT towards a gate and stile. Go through/over and continue AHEAD, ignoring a faint path going right. Pass another waymark. Soon, go RIGHT to a second waymark. Then bear RIGHT, following the main path downhill through some muddy patches to another waymark. Bear LEFT to a footpath sign alongside a road. Turn LEFT then RIGHT at another footpath sign.

6 Follow a waymarked path downhill. *The house to the left is Llwyniarth. Northwards you can see the upper Mawddach Valley and the mountains of northern Snowdonia.* Cross the stream, turn RIGHT and walk past a ruined house. Pass a waymark and go through a wooden gate to another waymark. Turn LEFT and pass two more waymarks. Then go LEFT across two streams and through a gateway. Walk downhill into trees. Pass a wooden gate (on the left) and then go AHEAD uphill on a rough path when the track turns right. Pass an old barn (on the left) when you start downhill across a field towards a telegraph pole AHEAD. Go LEFT of the pole to the waymark beyond it. Cross a stile and bridge then go AHEAD past a waymark.

7 Bear RIGHT and cross another bridge, then a stile by a gate and footpath sign. Go HALF-RIGHT towards a metal gate then HALF-RIGHT again to a stone stile and waymark. Go over onto a path which goes LEFT then RIGHT past a waymark then downhill to a wooden stile and waymark. Walk over and AHEAD to a waymark, gate and wooden stile. Cross this and walk AHEAD, over a stream then uphill. Go through an old gateway, LEFT past a waymark, then uphill again. Walk alongside a wall (on the right). Then go downhill, passing waymarks, into a gully. Ignore a track going left and bear RIGHT past a waymark. Make for a wall and stone stile alongside wooden posts. Once over, skirt a water channel. Then go LEFT downhill alongside the channel. Go LEFT onto a track and through a gate to a road and footpath sign.

8 Turn RIGHT and walk to a junction with a main road. Go RIGHT, past a post-box, walking on the RIGHT of this road. Soon, at speed restriction signs, cross the road and bear RIGHT over an old bridge. Go LEFT past a footpath sign and alongside a stream. Bear RIGHT past a footbridge and walk alongside the Wnion river. The path takes you back to the Marian car park. See **START** for the return route to Eldon Square bus stop

WALK 15

PEN Y BANC & PANDY'R ODYN

DESCRIPTION A 2-mile walk which provides some wonderful views over Dolgellau to the surrounding hills. It then takes you Pandy'r Odyn, on the western edge of the town, before you return alongside the fast-flowing river Wnion. Allow 1½ hours.

START Marian Mawr car-park near Dolgellau town-centre (SH 728179). From Eldon Square bus-stop turn LEFT (with your back to the bus-stop) and walk to Lombard Street. Turn RIGHT, then LEFT, past Y Sospan restaurant. Continue AHEAD, then go RIGHT, then LEFT down an alley-way past Yr Hên Efail tea-rooms.

DIRECTIONS Dolgellau can be reached from Porthmadog via the A487/A470, from Barmouth via the A496/A470, from Bala via the A494, from Machynlleth via the A487/A470, and from Tywyn via the A493. Park in the Marian Mawr car-park (SH 728179, post-code LL40 1UU) near the town-centre.

BUS SERVICES Buses 35 (from Blaenau Ffestiniog), 38 (from Barmouth), T2 (from Porthmadog and Machynlleth) and T3 (from Barmouth and Bala) serve Dolgellau. All buses stop in Eldon Square.

1 Walk to the car-park entrance near the bridge over the Wnion river. *The bridge is known as Y Bont Fawr and parts of it date from 1638. The bridge was seriously damaged when the Wnion flooded in 1903.* Cross the road at the bridge-end and continue AHEAD passing the old County Hall (on the right). *This impressive building dates from 1825 and continues in use as a court house. A slate at the front lists several local towns and villages.* Go through a metal gate into a park and bear HALF-LEFT. *Here you'll find a railway truck containing ore from Clogau Gold Mine, near Bontddu, a village on the Dolgellau-Barmouth road. (Walk 20 in 'Walks Around The Rhinogs' in the Kittiwake series takes you past Clogau Mine). Nearby in the park is a wooden sculpture by Alan Mantle entitled Roots.*

2 Continue along the path next to the river. Follow it RIGHT past the Dolgellau war memorial. Turn LEFT when the path divides and go through a metal gate AHEAD past a playground. Cross a footbridge over the river Aran. *The Aran is Dolgellau's second river. It flows from high on the flanks of Cadair Idris and joins the Wnion river a short distance below the footbridge.* Go down steps to the Glan Wnion Leisure Centre. Turn RIGHT here and walk AHEAD across the Co-op car-park. Bear RIGHT at the end of this and follow the road LEFT to Aran Bridge. *The existing bridge here was built on top of the earlier, narrower bridge. This area was at the centre of Dolgellau's woollen and tanning industries.*

3 Go AHEAD across the road and continue alongside the river. Turn RIGHT onto a road and walk uphill. At a junction continue AHEAD past houses and a road on the right, then turn RIGHT at a footpath sign. Follow a path through a metal gate and over a footbridge to cross the Aran river for a second time. Walk uphill to a road and turn LEFT, then LEFT again at a junction. Ignore a bridleway sign pointing right and pass a road going left. Continue uphill past a new housing development.

4 Continue to a footpath sign pointing right. Go RIGHT here up some steps, over a stile and uphill on a path through a stand of beech trees. *There is a good viewpoint just after the trees. Looking over Dolgellau you can see Y Garn, one of the Rhinog mountain peaks, in the distance. To the right, there is the rounded summit of Foel Offrwm, the site of an ancient hill-fort.* Soon cross another stile (ignore the path going left here) and walk AHEAD to a gate and third stile. Go over, past footpath and bridleway signs, and walk downhill. *Dolgellau Church and the town centre are clearly visible from here.* Pass another bridleway sign and join a road, walking AHEAD past Pen y Banc house.

5 Follow the road past a gateway and LEFT past Bryn Ffridd. Ignore three signposted paths going right and pass the gateway to

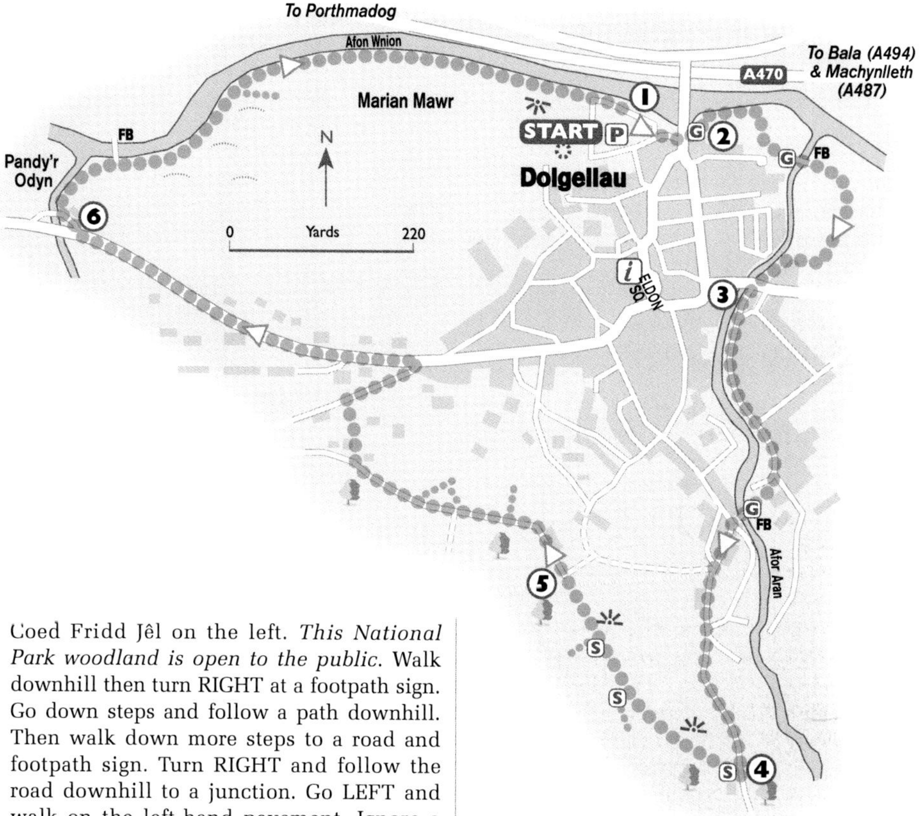

To Porthmadog
Afon Wnion
Marian Mawr
A470
To Bala (A494) & Machynlleth (A487)
START
Dolgellau
FB
Pandy'r Odyn
N
0 Yards 220
ELDON SQ
FB
Afor Aran

Coed Fridd Jêl on the left. *This National Park woodland is open to the public.* Walk downhill then turn RIGHT at a footpath sign. Go down steps and follow a path downhill. Then walk down more steps to a road and footpath sign. Turn RIGHT and follow the road downhill to a junction. Go LEFT and walk on the left-hand pavement. Ignore a road going left and continue until the footpath stops at a house. Cross the road here and go LEFT to an old bridge and footpath sign. *You are now at Pandy'r Odyn on the western outskirts of Dolgellau. The old bridge was closed to traffic in the mid-1920s.*

6 Turn RIGHT and follow a path alongside a stream. Bear RIGHT where the stream joins the Wnion river and walk past the ramp to a footbridge. Continue AHEAD on a path alongside the Wnion. *To the right is Dolgellau's main green space, the Marian Mawr. The stone circle you can see was created for the 1949 National Eisteddfod. There are good views from the path of Mynydd Moel, the easternmost peak of Cadair Idris, which towers above Dolgellau to the south.* The path takes you back to the Marian carpark.

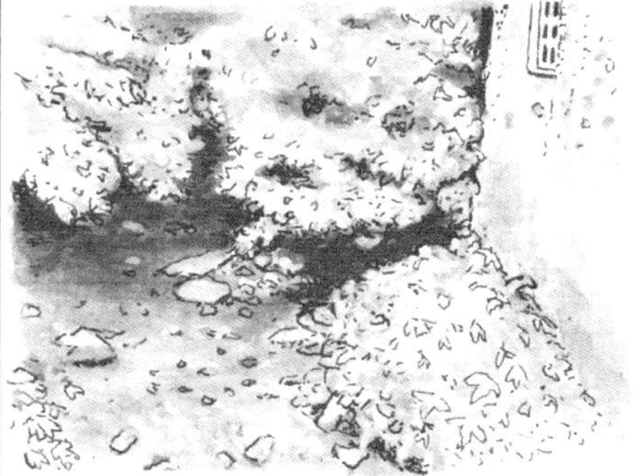

Afon Aran

WALK 16

PENTRE FARM & CYMER ABBEY

DESCRIPTION A 3-mile walk which takes you across Dolgellau's golf-course from where there are remarkable views down the Mawddach Valley. You then visit the ancient ruins of Cymer Abbey before walking to Llanelltyd Bridge, a fine old bridge over the Mawddach river. Allow 3 hours.

START Marian Mawr car-park near Dolgellau town-centre (SH 728179). From Eldon Square bus-stop turn LEFT (with your back to the bus-stop) and walk to Lombard Street. Turn RIGHT, then LEFT, past Y Sospan restaurant. Continue AHEAD, then go RIGHT, then LEFT down an alley-way past Yr Hên Efail tea-rooms.

DIRECTIONS Dolgellau can be reached from Porthmadog via the A487/A470, from Barmouth via the A496/A470, from Bala via the A494, from Machynlleth via the A487/A470, and from Tywyn via the A493. Park in the Marian Mawr car-park (SH 728179, post-code LL40 1UU) near the town-centre.

BUS SERVICES Buses 35 (from Blaenau Ffestiniog), 38 (from Barmouth), T2 (from Porthmadog and Machynlleth) and T3 (from Barmouth and Bala) serve Dolgellau. All buses stop in Eldon Square.

1 Walk to the car-park entrance then turn LEFT and cross the bridge over the river Wnion. *The bridge is called Y Bont Fawr and parts of it date from 1638. It was seriously damaged when the Wnion flooded in 1903.* At the end of the bridge turn LEFT then go RIGHT across the road at the pedestrian lights. Go LEFT then RIGHT into the first road on the right. Follow this road uphill, ignoring minor roads going off to left and right. After a time go through the end of speed limit signs and LEFT at a junction, joining a road signposted for the golf-course. *Look back here for a wonderful view over Dolgellau to the Cadair Idris ridge. The peak directly above Dolgellau is Mynydd Moel and the summit of the mountain, to the right of Mynydd Moel, is Penygadair. A seat is provided at this point for walkers who wish to rest and admire the view.*

2 Pass a house (on the right) and walk downhill past the golf-course car-park where the tarmac ends. Continue AHEAD on a track passing a waymark, and paths and tracks going to left and right. Just before a metal gate go RIGHT through a wooden gate opposite the entrance to Hengwrt Cottage. Bear LEFT, walking near a wall and fence on the left. *You are now on a right-of-way across the Dolgellau Golf-Course. The golf club here was established in 1910. Prominent in the distance ahead of you is Y Garn, a mountain in the Rhinog range. To the left there is a wonderful view down the Mawddach Valley towards Penmaenpool (see Walk 7).*

3 Pass a wooden post and walk downhill, past a white gas-line marker, to cross a stream on a wooden footbridge. Walk LEFT, ignoring a path going ahead, towards a metal gate. Turn RIGHT just before the gate and walk uphill alongside the wall. The path levels off and continues to another gate. Go through and walk to the right of Pentre farmhouse past a barn. Turn RIGHT after a metal gate on the right, and walk downhill to a road junction and footpath sign. Go LEFT and downhill to another junction, and footpath sign pointing left. Turn RIGHT then RIGHT again, opposite a signpost for Cymer Abbey, through a gateway onto the road to Vanner Caravan Park.

4 Pass a gate and track going right, and continue to a junction of tracks by a wall. Walk to the RIGHT, then go through a gateway and bear LEFT across a car-park. Go RIGHT through a metal gate to Cymer Abbey. *The abbey is just south of the village of Llanelltyd. 'Cymer' means 'confluence' and the abbey was built on the banks of the Mawddach river near its confluence with the Wnion, which flows from Dolgellau. The ruins date from the early 13thC. The abbey was one of the poorest Cistercian houses in Wales, with only five monks in 1388. It was dissolved in 1537.*

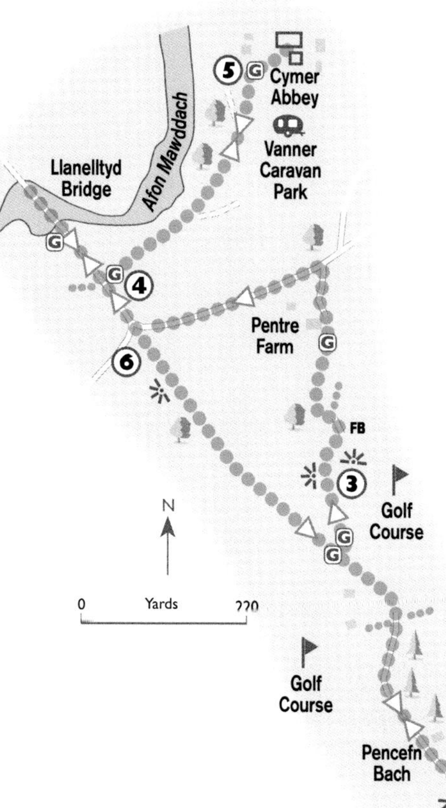

5 Return through the caravan park and turn RIGHT at the entrance. Walk the short distance, passing a car-park, to the old bridge over the Mawddach river. *The bridge dates from the mid-18th Century and has five elliptical arches. It was closed to traffic during the 1980s when a new bridge was built to the west of it, as you can see, to carry traffic on the A470 trunk road. There are gates to the riverside meadows on the left just before the bridge.* Retrace your steps past the caravan park entrance to the road junction and footpath sign beyond it. Walk AHEAD to join the signposted footpath. The path soon crosses a stream. *To the left here are the remains of an unusual field barn. On the right there's a gate from where there's a fine view of the upper Mawddach Estuary.*

6 Continue through an old gateway and, soon, reach a metal gate and kissing-gate. Go through, passing a gate on the left (through which you walked earlier) and Hengwrt Cottage. Continue on what is now a track. Pass a footpath sign and ignore paths and tracks going to left and right before joining a tarmac road. From here retrace your steps to the starting point.

Cymer Abbey

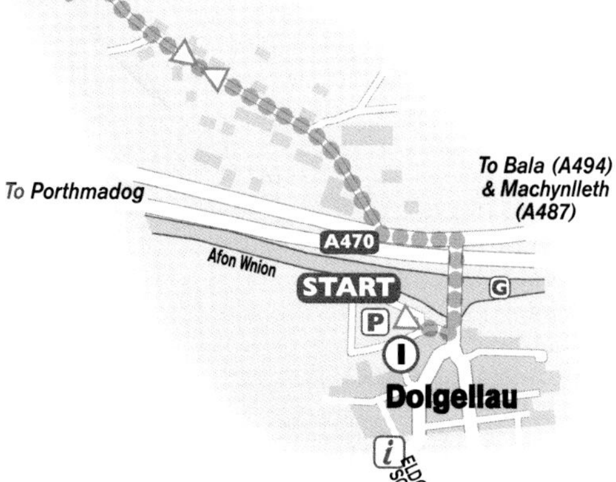

WALK 17

PANDY GADER & HAFODYGOESWEN

DESCRIPTION A 2½-mile walk during which you pass some old settlements which nestle, amidst spectacular scenery, below the towering ramparts of Mynydd Moel on the eastern ridge of Cadair Idris. Allow 2½ hours.

START Parking space on minor road above Plas y Brithdir (SH 737166, post-code LL40 1TE).

DIRECTIONS To Dolgellau: See Walk 1. From the Marian car-park: Turn RIGHT at the car-park exit and follow the one-way system. Go LEFT at a junction and over a bridge. Pass the entrance to Ysgol y Gader (on the right) and turn RIGHT into Fron Serth. Drive uphill, ignoring left and right turns. When Fron Serth bears left, go RIGHT, at a junction. Ignore a right turn into a housing estate. Then follow the narrow road uphill, turning sharp RIGHT past Plas y Brithdir farm (on the right). Go sharp LEFT over a bridge. After the gateway to Dref Gerrig (on the left) go LEFT at a junction and park near a phone-box.

From Eldon Square bus-stop: Follow Walk 2, Stages 1-4 to reach the START and Walk 2, Stages 5-7 to return to Dolgellau after completing Walk 17.

BUS SERVICES See Walk 2

1 With your back to the phone-box walk LEFT and follow the road signposted Cycle Route 21 uphill. Pass a footpath sign and house, Ty Cae Newydd, on the left. *This was a school from 1882-1972. The rights-of-way which converge at this point today no doubt survive from when local children walked to school here.* Immediately go RIGHT at another footpath sign and through a metal gate. Pass Pandy Gader house, going HALF-RIGHT, through a metal gate and over a footbridge to footpath signs. *You have just crossed the Aran, a river which flows steeply downhill to Dolgellau from its source high on Cadair Idris. Several of the mills associated with Dolgellau's woollen industry, including Pandy Gader, were located on the banks of the Aran.*

2 Turn LEFT and walk uphill, passing an old ford across the river and some ruined buildings. Follow the road RIGHT, passing field entrances. Walk through a wooden gate and AHEAD past Hafodygoeswen farm. Turn RIGHT through a small metal gate. Walk AHEAD across a rather boggy field and cross a stone stile by a footpath sign.

3 With your back to the stile, walk AHEAD parallel with the wall on the right. Go downhill to a waymark in trees. Walk through a gap in the wall, RIGHT down steps, then LEFT uphill to another waymark. Go through a wall and HALF-RIGHT to join a track coming in from the left. Go downhill, through a wall and alongside a fence behind a house. Go between the house and a telegraph pole (with waymark pointing RIGHT). Turn RIGHT and walk between the house, Pant yr Onnen, and a barn.

4 Pass the house entrance and then another barn (on the left). Go LEFT immediately after the barn and walk alongside a wall. Bear RIGHT at a water-course and follow this to a bridge. Go LEFT over this past another telegraph pole (on the left). Make for a gate and waymark AHEAD. Go through, over a stream then uphill. Continue AHEAD on an old track (ignore a minor track going right) with telegraph wires on the right. Pass a telegraph pole and go through a gap in a wall. Then go AHEAD, making for a gap in another wall to the left of another pole. *The house ahead of you is Coed Croes. The mountain in the distance is Y Garn, one of the Rhinog range.*

5 Go through the wall, past a building then turn RIGHT onto a track. Ignore a waymark pointing left and turn RIGHT onto a road. When the road bears left, go RIGHT across a wooden footbridge. Turn RIGHT through a wall and then LEFT alongside it past a waymark on a tree. Go RIGHT next to a gap in the wall and uphill past another waymark (on a tree on the left). Follow the path through trees, going HALF-LEFT, then RIGHT through a low wall. Turn RIGHT through another wall. Go LEFT uphill alongside the wall, then between the wall and a rocky outcrop on the right. Walk AHEAD parallel with the wall and a line of trees. Then bear HALF-RIGHT to go through a wall and past a ruined barn (on the right) to a track.

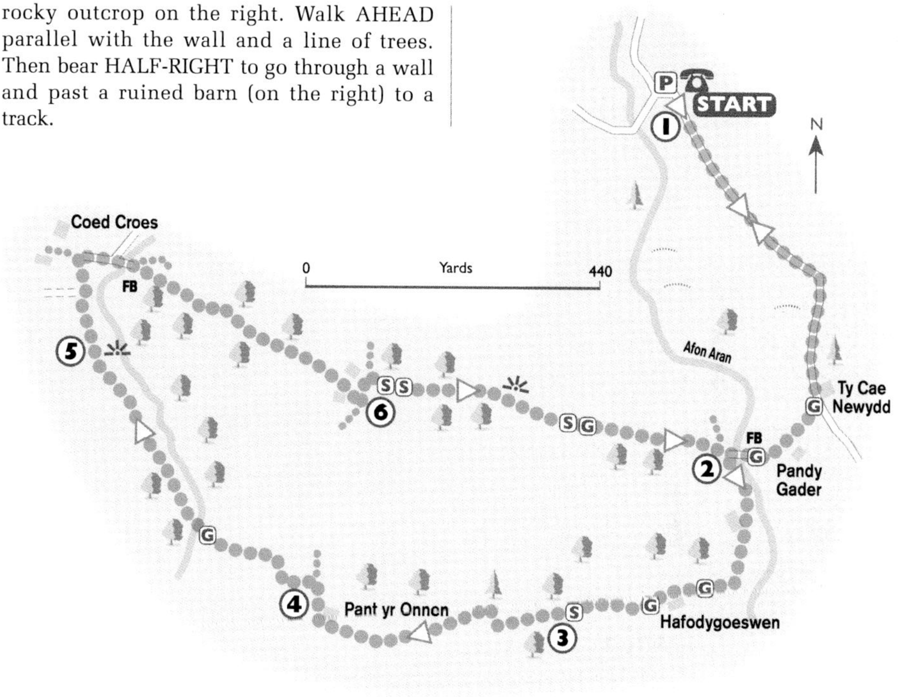

P START 1 N
Coed Croes
FB
0 Yards 440
5
6
Afon Aran
Ty Cae Newydd
FB
2
Pandy Gader
4
Pant yr Onnen
3
Hafodygoeswen

6 Turn LEFT then go RIGHT alongside the end wall of a second barn. Walk AHEAD to a stream. Cross this and go over two wooden stiles. Follow the path uphill through trees. Pass a waymark and a gate in the wall on the left. *There is a good view from the gate of the dome-shaped Rhobell Fawr, a mountain to the north-east of Dolgellau.* Continue alongside the wall then go LEFT over a stone stile in the wall and through a wooden gate. Continue AHEAD towards a ruined barn. Walk to the RIGHT of it, then bear HALF-RIGHT across a field towards a footpath sign. Go through a low wall and turn RIGHT onto a road. Then go LEFT over the footbridge near Pandy Gader. Retrace your steps to the starting point. ***Those returning to Dolgellau on foot should continue past the phone-box (with the phone-box on their right) to follow Walk 2, Stages 5-7.***

Pant yr Onnen

WALK 18

DREF GERRIG & TREFEILIA

DESCRIPTION This 3-mile walk takes you past some old settlements which were associated with the Quakers, who were once prominent as a religious group in the Dolgellau area. The route offers some wonderful views over the town and takes you alongside a precipitous stretch of the Aran river. Allow 3 hours.

START Parking space on minor road above Plas y Brithdir (SH 737166, post-code LL40 TE).

DIRECTIONS To Dolgellau: See Walk 1. From the Marian car-park: Turn RIGHT at the car-park exit and bear LEFT, following the one-way system. Turn LEFT when the road divides and drive over a bridge. Continue past the entrance to Ysgol y Gader (on the right) and immediately turn RIGHT into Fron Serth. Follow Fron Serth uphill, ignoring left and right turns. When Fron Serth bears left, go RIGHT at a junction. Ignore a right-turn into a housing estate. Then follow the narrow road uphill, turning sharp RIGHT past Plas y Brithdir farm (on the right) and then sharp LEFT over a bridge. After the gateway to Dref Gerrig (on the left) go LEFT at a junction and park off the road near a phone-box.

From Eldon Square bus-stop: Follow Walk 2, Stages 1-4 to reach the START and Walk 6, Stages 5-6 to return to Dolgellau after completing Walk 18, Stages 1-5.

BUS SERVICES See Walk 2

1 With your back to the phone-box go RIGHT downhill to a wooden gate (on the right). This is the entrance to Dref Gerrig (shown as Gerig on the OS map). Go through onto the road beyond and bear RIGHT when this divides. Continue uphill then go through a metal gate. *There is a good view from here back over Dolgellau to the Rhinog Mountains to the north-west.* Ignore three paths (two sign-posted) going right as you walk uphill to the road-end, next to a footpath sign and Dref Gerrig house. Go LEFT at the footpath sign and follow the waymarked path through a metal gate between the house and a barn to a stile. *There is a good view of a remarkable landscape from here. The dome-shaped mountain in the distance, on the right, is Rhobell Fawr, to the north-east of Dolgellau.*

2 Return to the footpath sign and turn LEFT onto what is now a track. Follow this uphill alongside a wall then bear RIGHT, ignoring a path going ahead, and go LEFT to join a forestry track. Soon, go through/over a wooden gate/stile and follow the track

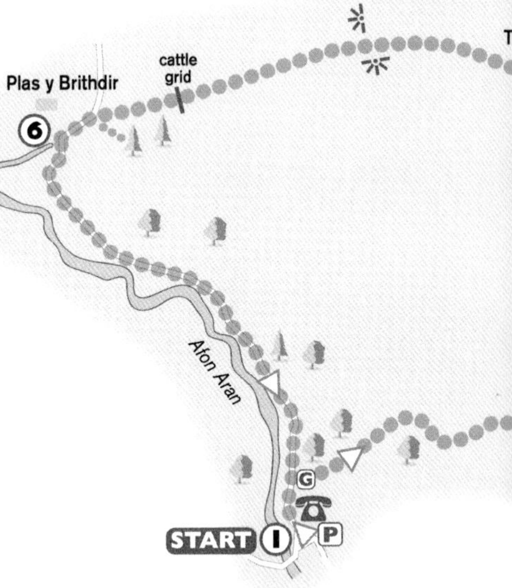

RIGHT uphill alongside a wall on the left. Ignore a footpath sign pointing right and follow the track downhill to an information board on the left. *Beyond the locked gate here are the ruins of Dewisbren Uchaf, during the 17thC a centre of Quakerism and the home of Dorothy Owen, a famous Quaker preacher.*

3 Continue along the track (ignoring a path going right) until you see a metal gate on the left. Leave the track and go through the gate past another notice-board to a road. Cross the road to the gate to Tabor Chapel and graveyard. *This chapel was once a Quaker meeting house. Persecuted during the 17thC, the Quakers fled from the Dolgellau area to America.* With your back to the chapel gate turn RIGHT and, ignoring a

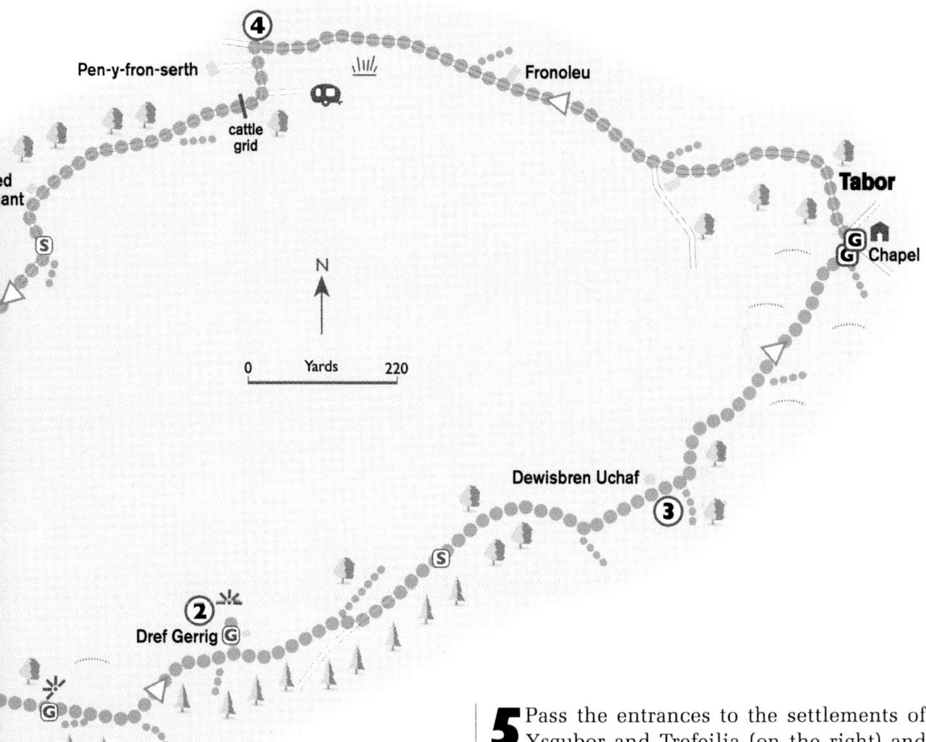

right-turn, follow the road uphill past a post-box. The road goes LEFT and downhill past the gateway to Coed and then the Fronoleu hotel (both on the right).

4 Turn LEFT onto a track opposite a bridleway sign. Ignore a track going right and follow the main track RIGHT past the entrance to Hafodlas caravan park. Cross a cattle-grid and continue on the track, past Coed Ceunant house and a barn, to a footpath sign on the right. Go RIGHT here, walking downhill and RIGHT over a wooden stile. Follow a path downhill, passing a gate, waymark and telegraph-poles (on the left) before reaching a wooden gate. Cross a stile to the left of the gate and walk downhill alongside a stream to a waymark. Turn LEFT, follow a track RIGHT and go through a wooden gate alongside a house.

5 Pass the entrances to the settlements of Ysgubor and Trefeilia (on the right) and continue AHEAD on a road, going through an old gateway and across fields. *Look to the left here for views of the eastern end of the Cadair Idris ridge and, ahead, of the Mawddach Estuary.* Soon, cross a cattle-grid and follow the road alongside a stream. At a road-junction and bridleway sign bear LEFT and follow the road past Plas y Brithdir Farm (on the right). ***Those returning to Dolgellau on foot should continue AHEAD after Plas y Brithdir, following Walk 6, Stages 5-6 past Frongoch house.***

6 Follow the road LEFT over a stream. Ignore a footpath sign pointing right and walk uphill. *The river to your right as you walk is the Aran which, as you can see, makes a precipitous journey downhill on its way to the centre of Dolgellau. Several of the mills associated with the local woollen industry were located on the banks of the Aran.* Pass the gateway to Tref Gerrig and retrace your steps to the starting point.

WALK 19

COED CROES & BRYN MAWR

DESCRIPTION A 3-mile walk during which you explore the area near Bryn Mawr house, above Dolgellau, once an important Quaker settlement. The views are spectacular, and the woodland you'll walk through is idyllic and interspersed with fast-flowing streams. Allow three hours.

START Parking space on minor road above Plas y Brithdir (SH 737166, post-code LL40 1TE).

DIRECTIONS To Dolgellau: See Walk 1. From the Marian car-park: Turn RIGHT at the car-park exit and bear LEFT, following the one-way system. Turn LEFT when the road divides and drive over a bridge. Continue past the entrance to Ysgol y Gader (on the right) and immediately turn RIGHT into Fron Serth. Follow Fron Serth uphill, ignoring left and right turns. When Fron Serth bears left, bear RIGHT at a junction. Ignore a right-turn into a housing estate. Then follow the narrow road uphill, turning sharp RIGHT past Plas y Brithdir farm (on the right) and then sharp LEFT over a bridge. After the gateway to Dref Gerrig (on the left) go LEFT at a junction and park off the road near a phone-box.

From Eldon Square bus-stop: Follow Walk 2, Stages 1-3 and go RIGHT at the footpath sign soon after Parc Cottage (see Stage 2 below). Then follow Walk 3, Stages 6-7 to return to Dolgellau after completing Walk 19, Stage 6 (see below).

BUS SERVICES See Walk 2.

1 With your back to the phone-box go AHEAD downhill to a junction and over a bridge. *This crosses the Aran, a river which descends precipitously from here to the centre of Dolgellau. Several fulling mills (for washing wool and cloth) were located on the banks of the Aran.* Go through the gate next to a cattle-grid and continue on the road. Ignore a track going left to Hafodygoeswen (see Walk 17) and go through a gate.

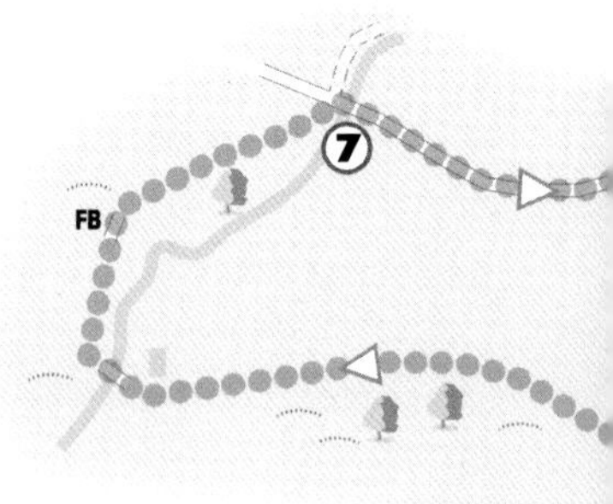

2 Turn LEFT onto a track at a footpath sign. Walk uphill to a waymark, go LEFT up some steps and over a stile. Continue HALF-RIGHT on the path beyond, ignoring a path going left. Pass another waymark and continue alongside a low wall. Go HALF-LEFT near a large boulder and alongside a higher wall to a waymark and stile. Go over and turn RIGHT onto a road. *The river to the left is the Aran again.*

3 Walk RIGHT to a footpath sign, go up steps and through a wall. Go AHEAD, then RIGHT after a ruined barn. Continue to a gate in a wall AHEAD. Go through, over a stile, and AHEAD. Pass a gate (on the right) and a waymark, then go downhill. Cross two wooden stiles, then a stream. Look AHEAD for the end-wall of a ruined barn. Walk towards it, turning LEFT onto a track just before it. Then go RIGHT and pass a second ruined barn. Walk through a gap in the wall AHEAD.

4 Bear HALF-RIGHT towards a line of trees and wall. Turn LEFT near the wall and walk parallel with it. Soon, go between a rocky outcrop and the wall. Walk RIGHT through a gateway in the wall then LEFT through a gateway in the low wall at right-angles to it. Go downhill on a faint path then bear HALF-RIGHT. Continue downhill past a waymark on a tree (to the right). Go LEFT before a gap in a low wall ahead. Walk alongside the wall past another waymark. Then go RIGHT through the wall and LEFT across a footbridge. Continue to a road. Go LEFT uphill to Coed Croes.

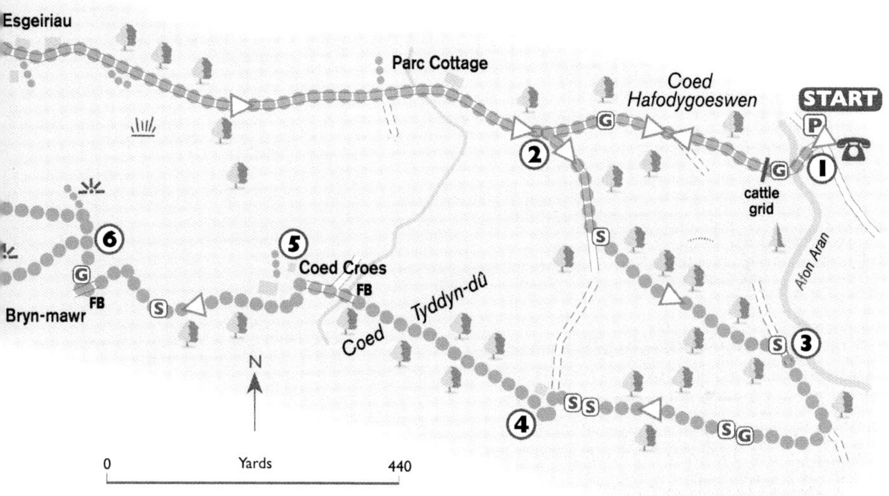

5 Turn LEFT, then RIGHT at a waymark and walk downhill behind the original farm-house. Pass more waymarks and go down steps to a track. Turn LEFT and cross a stream. Pass more waymarks and cross a stile. Go HALF-RIGHT across a field towards a gate and waymark. Cross a bridge, go through the gate and RIGHT onto the track beyond. Walk downhill to a waymark. *Go LEFT here to walk uphill to the gate of Bryn Mawr farmhouse, where there is an information board, and also wonderful views of the Rhinog mountains to the north. Bryn Mawr was the home of Rowland Ellis, a prominent Quaker, who emigrated to Pennsylvania in 1686. The American college and community of Bryn Mawr are named after the house.* Return to the junction of tracks and bear LEFT.

6 Walk past a barn to another waymark. *The mountain you can see ahead of you in the distance is Y Garn, one of the Rhinog range.* Go LEFT, walking towards a telegraph pole and old gateway. Pass two barns, ignoring a track going left. Walk downhill and cross a stream. Go through two old gateways then AHEAD, passing a ruin (on the right). Turn LEFT through a way-marked gateway, then go RIGHT. Cross a wider stream where there was once a ford. Walk uphill to a waymark and turn RIGHT, following the track from the ford. Continue alongside a fence to a waymark, then bear LEFT over a footbridge. Walk HALF-RIGHT uphill to another waymark. Continue towards some telegraph poles and another waymark. Then walk to a road and bridleway sign. ***Those returning to Dolgellau on foot should go through the metal gate opposite, following Walk 3, Stages 6-7.***

7 Turn RIGHT onto the road and follow it back to the starting point. You will go through a metal gate near Esgeiriau house and pass Parc Cottage on the way.

WALK 20

PEN YR ALLT & COED DREF GERRIG

DESCRIPTION This 2½-mile walk takes you to some remote settlements in and around woodland high on the eastern ridge of Cadair Idris. It visits some idyllic locations and offers some remarkable viewpoints. Allow 2½ hours.

START Parking space on minor road above Plas y Brithdir (SH 737166, post-code LL40 1TE).

DIRECTIONS To Dolgellau: See Walk 1. From the Marian car-park: Turn RIGHT at the car-park exit and follow the one-way system. Go LEFT at a junction and over a bridge. Pass the entrance to Ysgol y Gader (on the right) and turn RIGHT into Fron Serth. Drive uphill, ignoring left and right turns. When Fron Serth bears left, go RIGHT, at a junction. Ignore a right turn into a housing estate. Then follow the narrow road uphill, turning sharp RIGHT past Plas y Brithdir farm (on the right). Go sharp LEFT over a bridge. After the gateway to Dref Gerrig (on the left) go LEFT at a junction and park near a phone-box.

From Eldon Square bus-stop: Follow Walk 2, Stages 1-4 to reach the START and Walk 2, Stages 5-7 to return to Dolgellau after completing Walk 20.

BUS SERVICES See Walk 2

1 With your back to the phone-box, walk LEFT and follow the road (signposted Cycle Route 21) uphill. Continue to a footpath sign pointing left. Turn LEFT onto a path and pass a house, Ty Cae Newydd. *The house was a school from 1882-1972 and several paths meet at this point.* Follow the path across a grassy slope. *This area was cleared for the laying of a gas pipe-line, hence the white markers.*

2 Continue on a narrow path, crossing several streams. Soon, pass a ruined barn (to the right). *A glance behind you here will reveal the eastern summit of Cadair Idris, Mynydd Moel.* Follow the path through a wall, across another stream and through trees. Before long it descends to a road and a footpath sign. Turn RIGHT and follow the road over a stream then uphill. Ignore paths going right (the second signposted) before arriving at Dref Gerrig house (shown as Gerig on the OS map). The road ends here. Go LEFT at a footpath sign, following the way-marked path through a metal gate to a stile. *There is a good view from here over a remarkable landscape to Rhobell Fawr, the dome-shaped mountain to the north.*

3 *This short stage of the walk is optional in that you will return to the stile before continuing the walk. The stage takes you to the old settlement of Pen yr Allt and a nearby viewpoint.* Cross the stile and go RIGHT downhill alongside a fence. When the fence goes right continue AHEAD towards a stream and gateway in a wall.

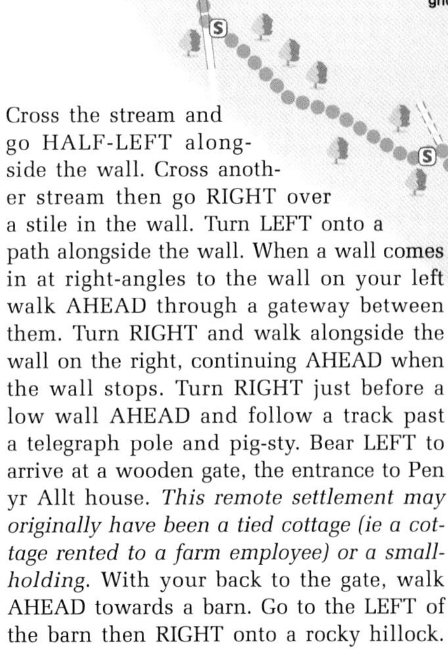

Cross the stream and go HALF-LEFT alongside the wall. Cross another stream then go RIGHT over a stile in the wall. Turn LEFT onto a path alongside the wall. When a wall comes in at right-angles to the wall on your left walk AHEAD through a gateway between them. Turn RIGHT and walk alongside the wall on the right, continuing AHEAD when the wall stops. Turn RIGHT just before a low wall AHEAD and follow a track past a telegraph pole and pig-sty. Bear LEFT to arrive at a wooden gate, the entrance to Pen yr Allt house. *This remote settlement may originally have been a tied cottage (ie a cottage rented to a farm employee) or a smallholding.* With your back to the gate, walk AHEAD towards a barn. Go to the LEFT of the barn then RIGHT onto a rocky hillock.

The mountain view from here is spectacular. To the left is Diffwys, ahead is Y Garn (both mountains in the Rhinog range). Half-right is Rhobell Fawr, and right are the Aran mountains. Retrace your steps to Dref Gerrig.

4 Return to the road and turn RIGHT. After a short distance go LEFT at a footpath sign and follow a path uphill through trees. Cross a stream then turn LEFT at a waymark. Go RIGHT onto a forestry track at the next waymark and walk uphill. Bear RIGHT at a junction, passing another waymark on the left. *You are now in Coed Dref Gerrig, a large forestry plantation which reaches a height of over 300m on the north-eastern slopes of Cadair Idris.* Go through a metal gate to a road and cycle-track sign.

5 Turn RIGHT and follow the road downhill. Turn LEFT at a footpath sign and go through a metal gate. Walk downhill, past Pandy Gader house, going HALF-RIGHT, through a metal gate and over a footbridge to another footpath sign.Turn RIGHT onto the road beyond and walk downhill, ignoring a footpath sign pointing left. Go through a wall and immediately LEFT at a waymark. Cross a stile and walk AHEAD on a path between trees. Bear HALF-RIGHT, pass a waymark and walk alongside a wall (on the left). Pass another waymark and go downhill to a stile. Walk over and down steps past a waymark to a track. Go RIGHT downhill to a road and footpath sign. Turn RIGHT and follow the road through a metal gate. Ignore a track going right to Hafodygoeswen (see Walk 17). Then go through the gate alongside a cattle-grid and cross the river Aran. Go RIGHT uphill to the starting point. ***Those returning to Dolgellau on foot should bear LEFT here, continuing on the road alongside the river to follow Walk 2, Stages 5-7.***

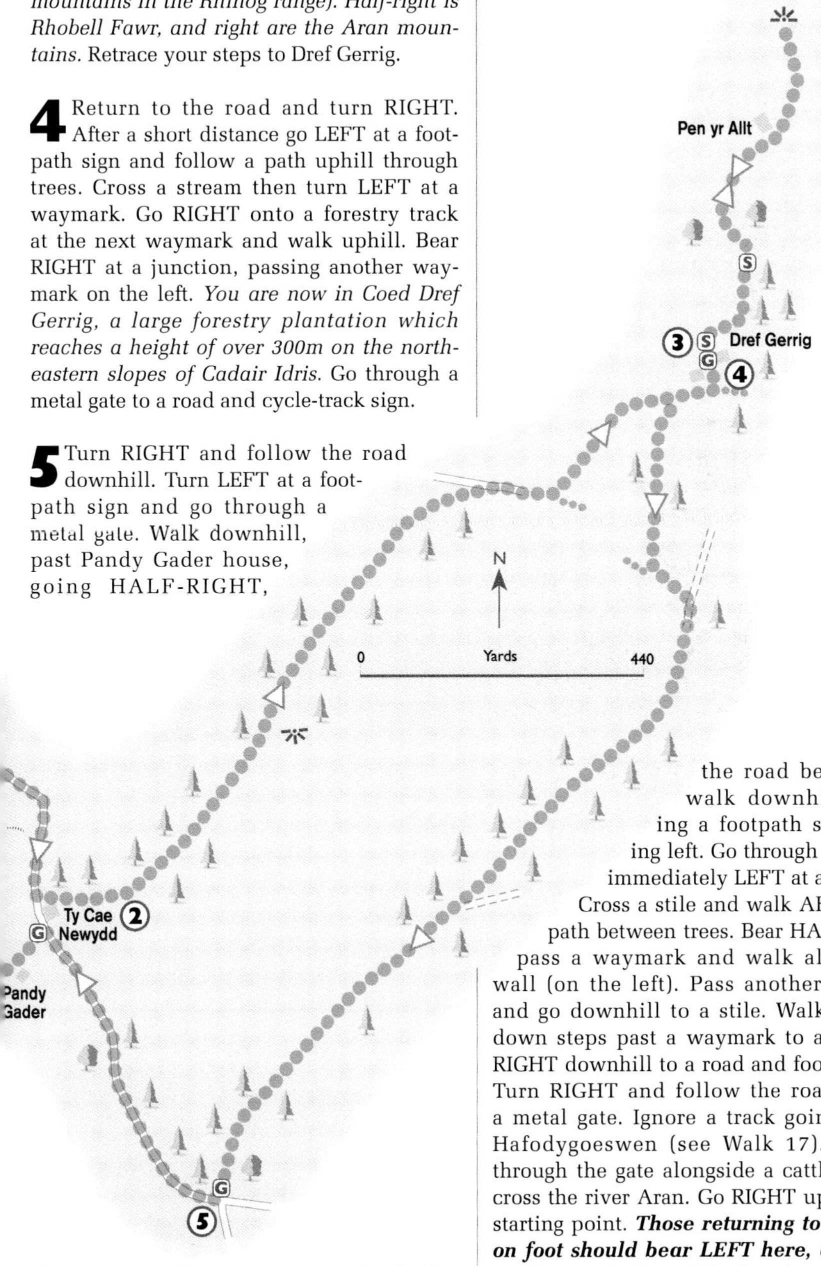

Summary of the walks

Walk number	Starting place	Grid reference of start	Length of walk (miles)	Grade – See below	Average time to allow for walk (hours)	Remarks
1	**Eldon Square BS**	SH728178	2	*M*	1½	Views, river, wood
2	**Marian CP**	SH728179	2½	*M*	2½	River, forest, views
3	**Eldon Square BS**	SH728178	2½	*M*	2½	Historic buildings, wood, views
4	**Marian CP**	SH728179	2	*M*	1½	Historic bridge, river, views
5	**Marian CP**	SH728179	2½	*M*	2	River, views, historic site
6	**Eldon Square BS**	SH728178	2½	*M*	2½	Views, woods, river, historic buildings
7	**Marian CP**	SH728179	5½	*S*	5	River, views, old railway line
8	**Eldon Square BS**	SH728178	1½	*E*	1½	Historic buildings, views, historic well, river, garden
9	**Eldon Square BS**	SH728178	1½	*E*	1½	Historic buildings,views, rivers, sculpture, park
10	**Marian CP**	SH728179	4	*M*	3½	River, views, Mawddach trail
11	**Eldon Square BS**	SH728178	4½	*S*	4½	Views, ruin, lake, forest
12	**Eldon Square BS**	SH728178	4½	*M*	4	River, wood, views, historic Quaker sites
13	**Eldon Square BS**	SH728178	4½	*M*	4	Historic buildings, historic well, views
14	**Eldon Square BS**	SH728178	4½	*S*	4½	Views, ruin, old bridge, river
15	**Marian CP**	SH728179	2	*E*	1½	Rivers, sculpture, views, stone circle
16	**Marian CP**	SH728179	3	*M*	3	River, views, abbey ruins, old bridge
17	**Above Plas y Brithdir**	SH737166	2½	*M*	2½	River, views, old mill site and settlements
18	**Above Plas y Brithdir**	SH737166	3	*M*	3	Views, historic Quaker sites, river
19	**Above Plas y Brithdir**	SH737166	3	*M*	3	River, views, old farm-house, historic Quaker site
20	**Above Plas y Brithdir**	SH737166	2½	*M*	2½	Views, old settlements, forest, river

Walk grading: *This is for guidance only. Few walks in this beautiful area are completely level.*

E – **Easy** Any uphill sections are short and not steep.

M – **Moderate** Involves some uphill walking, but easily managed by a reasonably fit person.

S – **Strenuous** Some long or steep uphill sections, but OK for a reasonably fit person.

CP = Car Park **BS** = Bus Stop

PRONUNCIATION

Welsh	*English equivalent*
c	always hard, as in **c**at
ch	as in the Scottish word lo**ch**
dd	as th in **th**en
f	as f in o**f**
ff	as ff in o**ff**
g	always hard as in **g**ot
ll	no real equivalent. It is like 'th' in then, but with an 'L' sound added to it, giving 'thlan' for the pronunciation of the Welsh 'Llan'.

In Welsh the accent usually falls on the last-but-one syllable of a word.

KEY TO THE MAPS

- Walk route and direction
- Metalled road
- Unsurfaced road
- Footpath/route adjoining walk route
- River/stream
- Trees
- Gate
- Stile
- Footbridge
- Viewpoint
- Parking
- Telephone

THE COUNTRYSIDE CODE

- Be safe – plan ahead and follow any signs
- Leave gates and property as you find them
- Protect plants and animals, and take your litter home
- Keep dogs under close control
- Consider other people

Open Access

Some routes cross areas of land where walkers have the legal right of access under The CRoW Act 2000 introduced in May 2005. Access can be subject to restrictions and closure for land management or safety reasons for up to 28 days a year. Details from: www.naturalresourceswales.gov.uk.
Please respect any notices.

About the author, Michael Burnett...

Michael is a musician who has written articles and presented radio programmes about Welsh traditional music. He is also the author of four other Kittiwake guides: The Rhinogs, East of Snowdon, Coed y Brenin and Barmouth Town. His links to Wales go back to his teenage years when he regularly stayed with friends near Maentwrog and to the 1970s when he lived with his wife, Paula, and their two young children at Blaen Myherin, a remote farmhouse above Devil's Bridge which has now, sadly, become a ruin. Today Michael and Paula share an old farmhouse near the northern Rhinog ridge.

Michael would like to thank the following for their advice and support in the preparation of this book: The Public Rights of Way Unit at Gwynedd Council in Dolgellau, and Peter Jackson, Chairman of the Dolgellau Partnership.

Published by **Kittiwake-Books Limited**
3 Glantwymyn Village Workshops, Glantwymyn, Machynlleth, Montgomeryshire SY20 8LY

Drawings by Morag Perrott
Cover photos: Main: Dolgellau and Mynydd Moel.
Inset: Cymer Abbey. David Perrott

Printed by Mixam, UK.

ISBN: **978 1 908748 27 0**

KITTIWAKE

Walks guides which detail superb routes
in most parts of Wales & the Borders.

From Anglesey and Snowdonia to the Brecon Beacons, and from Machynlleth and Welshpool to Pembrokeshire and the Llŷn, including the Borders and Glamorgan, they offer a range of carefully researched routes with something for all abilities.

Each guide has been compiled and written by a dedicated author who really knows their particular area.

They are all presented in the **KITTIWAKE** clear and easy-to-use style

For latest details of the expanding range visit:

www.kittiwake-books.com

KITTIWAKE
3 Glantwymyn Village Workshops
Glantwymyn, Machynlleth
Montgomeryshire SY20 8LY